HI-FIDELITY

JAZZ

INSTRUMENTALS
& VOCALS

LONG-PLAYING

THE GOLDEN ERA

TWENTY CLASSIC JAZZ TRACKS

EDITION OLMS ZÜRICH

JAZZ

THE GOLDEN ERA

JAZZ

THE GOLDEN ERA

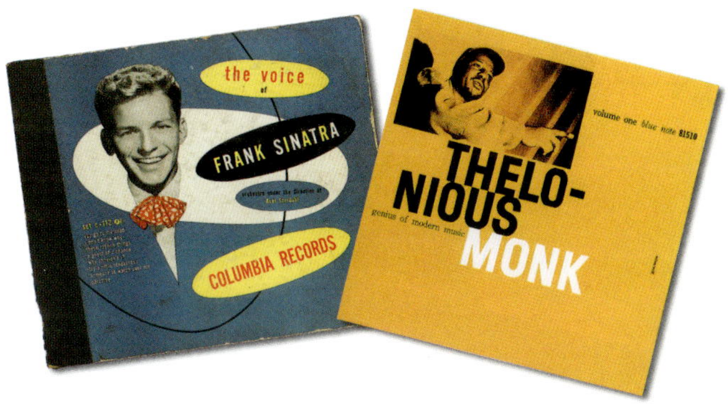

RICHARD HAVERS & RICHARD EVANS

EDITION OLMS ZÜRICH

Authorized edition 2010 for Germany,
Austria and Switzerland by

EDITION OLMS AG ZÜRICH
Willikonerstr. 10
CH-8618 Oetwil am See/Zürich
Switzerland
website: www.edition-olms.com
e-mail: info@edition-olms.com

ISBN 978-3-283-01149-9

Compiled, written and designed by
Richard Havers and Richard Evans.

Printed and bound in China

CONTENTS

CONCERT BY THE SEA
ERROLL GARNER
BIRTH OF THE COOL
miles davis
ILLINOIS JACQUET
COLUMBIA
COLLATES
ILLINOIS JACQUET
ROY AND DIZ
THELO-NIOUS MONK
GENE KRUPA
AND HIS ORCHESTRA
COLUMBIA RECORDS

William Gottlieb

When a photographer gets a great shot of a performer it's most often because they catch a moment on stage when something magical happens; to get great shots of performers in private is much more difficult. William Gottlieb managed to achieve both. All too often, when photographers take pictures of people, they fail to capture the essence of the person – they merely capture an image. William Gottlieb knew most of the musicians whose pictures he took; it's this that makes these pictures so remarkable.

William P. Gottlieb

He was born in Brooklyn, New York in 1917, which made him of similar age to many of the jazz greats that feature in his photography. Having grown up in New Jersey, where his father worked in the building business, William went to Lehigh University to study economics; both his parents died while he was a teenager. It was in 1936 while at Lehigh that he first became interested in jazz. Having been brought low by a bout of food poisoning, he spent much of the summer in bed listening to jazz records which had been supplied by a high school friend and chatting with him about "America's contribution to the arts."

On his return to university, Gottlieb began writing a regular column for *The Lehigh Review*, later becoming its editor-in-chief. On leaving university he got a job on the *Washington Post* selling advertising space. After a few months he persuaded them to let him write a weekly column about jazz; the *Post* agreed to pay him an extra $10 a week. Initially, a photographer went to jazz clubs and concerts with Gottlieb, but soon the *Post* decided this was an unnecessary expense. Anxious to continue to get pictures for his column, he traded some of his precious jazz records for a $3\frac{1}{4}$ x $4\frac{1}{4}$-inch Speed Graphic camera, film, and flashbulbs.

The camera was just like the ones that we're all used to seeing in classic Hollywood movies when photographers crowd around their victim. It all looks easy on film, but in reality using a Speed Graphic was a lot more complicated. Getting to grips with the new camera was a challenge. After just one afternoon's tuition from a *Post* photographer, William had no alternative but to teach himself. Because the Speed Graphic was limited to two exposures without reloading, it meant that he had to think through precisely what he wanted to take each time he used the camera. In addition, the film and flashbulbs were expensive, so there was none of the flexibility offered by modern digital photography. The result is quality, not quantity in William Gottlieb's work.

By the time war broke out he also had his own radio show in Washington DC that featured many of the great jazz musicians who passed through the capital. Other guests included his friends, Nesuhi and Ahmet Ertegun, both keen jazz fans as well as being the sons of the Turkish Ambassador to the United States. Ahmet Ertegun went on to co-found Atlantic Records. In 1941 William left his advertising job at the *Post*, deciding instead to teach at the University of Maryland. By 1943 he had been drafted into the Army Air Corps where he served as a photo officer.

With the war over, William settled in New York and got a job on *Down Beat* magazine as a reporter and reviewer, but he continued to take photographs; he was soon better known for his pictures than his writing. He also began working for *Record Changer* magazine, which also published many of his pictures. Many of his photographs were taken in the great jazz clubs that were to be found on 52nd Street or on 'Swing Street' the block between 5th and 6th Avenues.

By the end of the 1940s, having married and had children, William thought it time to settle down and get himself a regular job that would allow him to spend evenings at home, not out on the town with his jazz musician friends. He was offered a job at Curriculum Films, an educational filmstrip company. Later he started his own company, and when this was bought out by McGraw Hill he became a president of a division; it's where he stayed until he retired in 1979.

William Gottlieb died of a stroke in 2006. His work will be remembered as long as people listen to the music of the Golden Era of Jazz. Not least, because he captured people with a truth that almost no one else managed to achieve. His photographs capture the essence of the performers – which words alone cannot convey.

William P. Gottlieb writing for the Washington Post c. 1940.

JAZZ

"I don't have a definition of jazz... You're just supposed to know it when you hear it." *~ Thelonious Monk*

Jazz the "elixir of American life," the one pure American art form, is something that just is. It all began in New Orleans, the Crescent City, but there's no big bang theory; it didn't just appear out of nowhere. Jazz evolved from the music played and sung throughout the southern USA by the black population. Theirs were the plantation songs, field hollers, gospel songs, ragtime, folk tunes that were all mixed with a tinge of European music, and instruments played by musicians for an eager audience. That's what they called entertainment.

Canal Street, Storyville in the early 1920s.

In New Orleans, with its relatively sophisticated population, there was a crystallization of all these forms of music into jazz. The influence of the city's Creole population, its musical sophisticates, helped create this heady, exciting, musical mix. When the influx of rural blacks from the Mississippi Delta, bringing with them their blues songs, was added, it created magic.

At the beginning of the twentieth century the musical heart of New Orleans was Storyville, with Canal Street running through its centre along with Franklin Street, Rampart Street, Tulane Street and perhaps most famously Basin Street – all names inexorably associated with jazz. It was a bustling and vibrant area of saloons, clubs, brothels, theaters, churches, restaurants, shops, and businesses. Music helped to create a giddy atmosphere, scarcely replicated anywhere in the world before or since. In 1897 Storyville had been designated as the cities "tenderloin district," this was to segregate vice from the remainder of the city; a sort of sexual cleansing. Today's visitors can scarcely imagine the scenes.

Jazz evolved from ragtime, which had been an attempt by the black brothel pianists along Basin Street to emulate the city's brass bands. It was just one of the building

"Jazz is the big brother of the blues. If a guy's playing blues he's in high school. When he starts playing jazz it's like going on to college." ~ *BB King*

A Storyville "professional," early 1900s.

blocks of jazz – "the blackening of American musical grammar," as it's been called.

While there is little debate about where jazz started, there is plenty about how it got its name. It might have come from an itinerant black musician known as Jazbo Brown who played in the Delta; his audience would shout "more Jazbo, more Jaz." Some have argued that it's a corruption of the name of a New Orleans band known as Razz. Then again early bands were billed as "Jas" or "Jass" bands, which further confuses the issue. In any case, what's in a name?

Storyville created an almost inexhaustible demand for musicians: many of them were young, many of them black, and few could read music. In 1894 the city had enacted a segregation code that moved the Creoles to this uptown area of New Orleans. The more sophisticated Creole musicians influenced the younger, less experienced, black musicians. The best jazz bands in town were to be found in the better "professional houses" of the quarter, and very soon they were heard playing a form of jazz that became known as "hot jazz."

The first noteworthy exponent was Charles "Buddy" Bolden who started his band in the early 1890s. By 1895 he was acknowledged as the "King of the Trumpet," and his was reckoned to be the best of the hot bands. Bolden, unlike many of his contemporaries, could read music, but he preferred to play by ear, with his flair for natural jazz phrasing and spontaneity. Bolden primarily played parades and dances, and not surprisingly, his band included some of the best musicians. To modern ears Bolden's jazz seems less than adventurous, but it should be taken in context. Bolden freely embellished the melodies, pointing the way forward, and all the while producing those "fiery rhythms." Sometime around 1907 Bolden went mad while playing in a street parade; in 1931 he died, without ever regaining his sanity.

Most famous of Bolden's contemporaries was Willie "Bunk" Johnson, who played cornet with his band. Soon a second wave of outstanding jazzmen began appearing, such as trumpeters Freddie Keppard and Joseph "King"

The Buddy Bolden band in 1905.

"Jazz has always been the kind of man you wouldn't want your daughter to associate with." *~ Duke Ellington*

Oliver, trombonist Frank Dusen, along with clarinetists, George Baquet, Johnny Dodds and Sidney Bechet. Louis Armstrong, who was born in New Orleans at the turn of the century, learned from Bunk Johnson. Towards the end of the First World War, Armstrong was playing with Kid Ory, another of the new breed of jazzmen.

In 1908 Freddie Keppard's band toured America, the first band from New Orleans to do so. By 1913 they were known as the Original Creole Jazz Band, and for audiences it was their first exposure to this exciting new music. King Oliver, having played with Kid Ory's band, moved to Chicago around 1918, helping to spread the jazz sound in what was fast becoming the largest black population of any northern city. Ferdinand Joseph Morton was another born in the Crescent City. Jelly Roll Morton wound up in Chicago, having worked his way through the South as a solo pianist. Like many others, he too spread the gospel in his own unique way.

One reason for what seemed like a mass exodus of musicians from New Orleans was that the US Navy demanded that Storyville be closed in 1917. It truly was the end of an era, but curiously it coincided with a change that would spread the sound of jazz, and every other form of popular music, far faster than it took itinerant bands and musicians to travel around the country. Radio and recorded music, on 78-rpm records, were about to make music "mass market," forever, changing the face of entertainment. The Original Dixieland Jazz Band recorded the first jazz record, which was called "Livery Stable Blues" and the band were white, not black.

Throughout the twenties and thirties jazz took hold of not just America, but also Europe. Both Louis Armstrong and Duke Ellington travelled across the Atlantic from New York and were rapturously received. It was New York that had become the recording, and arguably, the jazz capital of the world, following the early development of jazz in Chicago, Kansas City and the other industrial cities with large black populations. The increasing popularity of the big bands was assisted by radio, with nightly broadcasts from the top New York hotels and ballrooms via their expanding networks. Clubs in New York were pivotal to the development of the music and particularly its evolution from big band swing into bop, be-bop, and the sound of modern jazz.

Perhaps most famous of all New York's jazz venues was the Cotton Club on West 142nd Street, which featured Duke Ellington's Famous Orchestra, both live and on radio. It exuded a racy, roaring twenties image, to which the Duke's jazz provided the soundtrack. Besides the Duke, the bands of Cab Calloway and Jimmie

"Jazz is an intensified feeling of nonchalance." *~ Françoise Sagan*

"Things were flexible on The Street. Don Byas might have an engagement at the Three Deuces as a leader and then he'd go next door to the Downbeat as a sideman with Coleman Hawkins." *~ Billy Taylor, the house pianist at Birdland*

Cab Calloway at the Cotton Club on West 142nd Street, New York

Lunceford played at the Cotton Club, helping it to become the epitome of the pre-war jazz age. Meanwhile, Chick Webb's band was at the Savoy, on Lennox Avenue between West 140th and 141st Streets; others bands were at Connee's Inn, just next to the Apollo Theater.

Shows at cinemas that featured bands, singers comedians, jugglers and acrobats, in addition to the movies, provided another showcase for jazz – often a whiter kind of jazz. It was the biggest of the big bands that played them – Benny Goodman, Tommy Dorsey or Woody Herman – who could gross as much as $50,000 a week by the late 1930s. Other bands such as Artie Shaw and Charlie Barnett dominated the hotels; all were featured on the radio.

Prohibition helped to create the club scene on 52nd Street, often using the basements of the brownstone buildings above. This was a different kind of jazz, almost underground, so that by the mid-thirties clubs including The Famous Door, The Hickory House, and The 21 Club were all in full swing. There was a segregation policy in operation, and while there was some mixing of the races it wasn't until Café Society opened in January 1939 that there was real integration. During the war years things were kept jumping on the streets of New York by those men who, for whatever reason, failed to make it into the services. But times were clearly changing.

It was the world of smoky, dimly lit, clubs playing every known form of jazz that William Gottlieb found himself frequenting in postwar New York City. The club scene laid down a musical soundtrack like no other; it was variety personified, from

Following page: 52nd Street, New York in July 1948. Some of the clubs on the street included the Three Deuces, The Onyx, Jimmy Ryan's, The 21 Club, Toots Shor, Leon and Eddies, The Bluenote, and the Club Carousel.

RYAN'S
BAR
TONY'S
ONYX
HARRY the HIPSTER
ONYX

CLUB
SAMOA
FINK
Club CAROUSEL
3 DEUCES
FAMOUS DOOR
B.S. PULLY
CLUB CAROUSEL
J.C. HEARD
OSCAR PETTIFORD
THREE DEUCES
THREE DEUCES Presents
ALL STAR QUARTET
J.C.HEARD
JACKIE PARIS

Sidney Bechet playing traditional jazz, to Charlie Parker and Dizzy Gillespie experimenting with bop. If anyone was noticing the changes in taste of the public then they hadn't necessarily told the musicians on 52nd Street or in Harlem. Jazz, like most other art forms, often reflects life, and it was economics that were behind the changing times. The swing bands cost a lot to keep on the road; there were a lot of mouths to feed. At the same time postwar construction would see the buildings on 52nd Street demolished to make way for brighter, bigger buildings. Jazz was also going mainstream; the radio had a lot to answer for.

In the late 1930s both Benny Goodman and Duke Ellington played New York's Carnegie Hall and the trend continued postwar. Charlie Parker played there, as did Woody Herman, and in 1949, *Jazz at the Philharmonic* established the Hall as its New York home. But it was still the clubs that were the haunt of the jazzmen. There was the Downbeat on West 52nd Street, which opened in 1944 and featured just about everyone before it became a strip club in 1948. Billie, Ella, Coleman and Dizzy were all there and Gottlieb caught Dizzy in performance at the club in 1947.

Café Society features in Gottlieb's photographs, both the downtown club at Sheridan Square, and the uptown club at 128 East 58th Street. Among those he photographed at the downtown club were Sarah Vaughan and Josh White. The Three Deuces at 72 West 52nd Street, on the site of the old Onyx club, is where he photographed, Flip Phillips, Coleman Hawkins, Max Roach, Charlie Parker, Jack Teagarden and Miles Davis.

Other clubs photographed by William Gottlieb include Minton's Playhouse on West 118th Street (which was run by former bandleader Teddy Hill in the 1940s), the Hickory House, one of 52nd Street's longest running venues, Kelly's Stables anther 52nd Street stalwart, Nick's Tavern on West 10th Street, the Spotlight Club on 52nd Street, the Village Vanguard on 7th Avenue, and Eddie Condon's on West 3rd Street. It may not be not every New York club, that feature in his photography, but it's not far short.

Birdland, one of New York's most famous venues, did not open until December 1949, by which time Gottlieb had given up hanging out in the clubs and got himself a "proper job" as he had the responsibility of raising a family. The old guard was starting to move over to make way for those intent on playing jazz their way: jazz, like all art, evolves and develops. But thankfully, that was not before William Gottlieb captured the best ever collection of jazz photographs. We're just fortunate he was there to capture jazz during its golden era.

Sarah Vaughan singing at Café Society, Downtown, New York, c. August 1946.

A JAZZ TIMELINE

1897 Storyville in New Orleans opens.

1898 Ragtime is all the rage.

1900 The blues becomes increasingly popular.

1902 Jelly Roll Morton developing jazz style piano.

1903 W.C. Handy hears the blues in Tutwiler, Mississippi.

1910 Joe Oliver plays professionally in Storyville.
In New York, James Reece Europe's Clef Club opens to promote interests in black musicians.

1911 Kid Ory and Armand Piron are leading bands in New Orleans.

1912 Alexander's Ragtime Band is recorded by bands in London.
W.C. Handy publishes "Memphis Blues."

1913 Freddie Keppard's Original Creole Band begins touring the USA.

1914 W.C. Handy publishes "St. Louis Blues."
Louis Mitchell's Southern Syncopated Quintet play ragtime in London.

1915 Jelly Roll Morton publishes "Jelly Roll Blues."

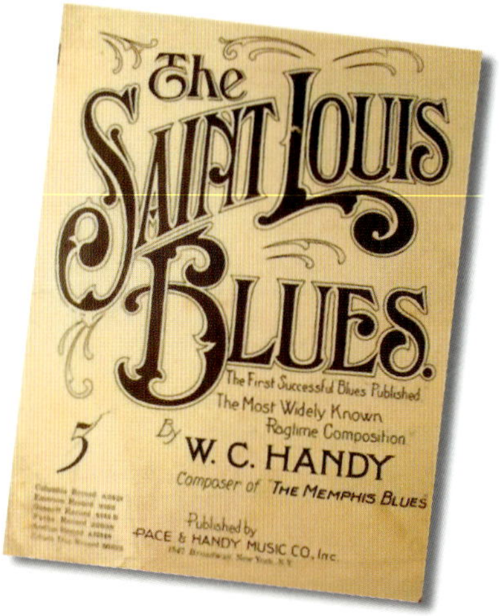

1916 Johnny Stein's Dixie Jass band, from New Orleans, performs in Chicago.
Nick La Rocca's band becomes the Original Dixieland Jass Band.

1917 Original Dixieland Jazz Band perform in New York and record "Livery Stable Blues," the first jazz record.

1918 James Reese Europe's "Hellfighters" touring France.
Joe Oliver moves to Chicago, and Louis Armstrong replaces Oliver in Kid Ory's Band.

1919 The Original Dixieland Jazz Band performs at the London Hippodrome and Palladium.
The Southern Syncopated Orchestra is in Europe with clarinetist, Sidney Bechet.

1920 Paul Whiteman records for HMV.

1921 James P. Johnson records first piano solos.

1922 Louis Armstrong moves to Chicago.

1923 King Oliver's Creole Jazz Band first record for Gennett.
Jelly Roll Morton records piano solos.
Paul Whiteman Orchestra performs in London.

1924 Wolverines, with Bix Beiderbecke record.

Louis Armstrong records with Fletcher Henderson Orchestra.

1925 Louis Armstrong's Hot Five make first record.

1926 Jelly Roll Morton and his Red Hot Peppers record for Victor.
Paul Whiteman Orchestra featuring George Gershwin playing *Rhapsody In Blue,* visit Britain.

1927 Duke Ellington records "Black And Tan Fantasy" and appears at the Cotton Club.
Meade Lux Lewis records "Honky Tonk Train Blues."

1928 Benny Goodman's Boys record.
Dorsey Brothers' Orchestra records.
Louis Armstrong's Hot Five record "West End Blues."

1929 "Handful Of Keys" begins Fats Waller's series of solo piano recordings.
Film *St. Louis Blues* stars Bessie Smith
Ellington band appear in film short *Black and Tan Fantasy*.

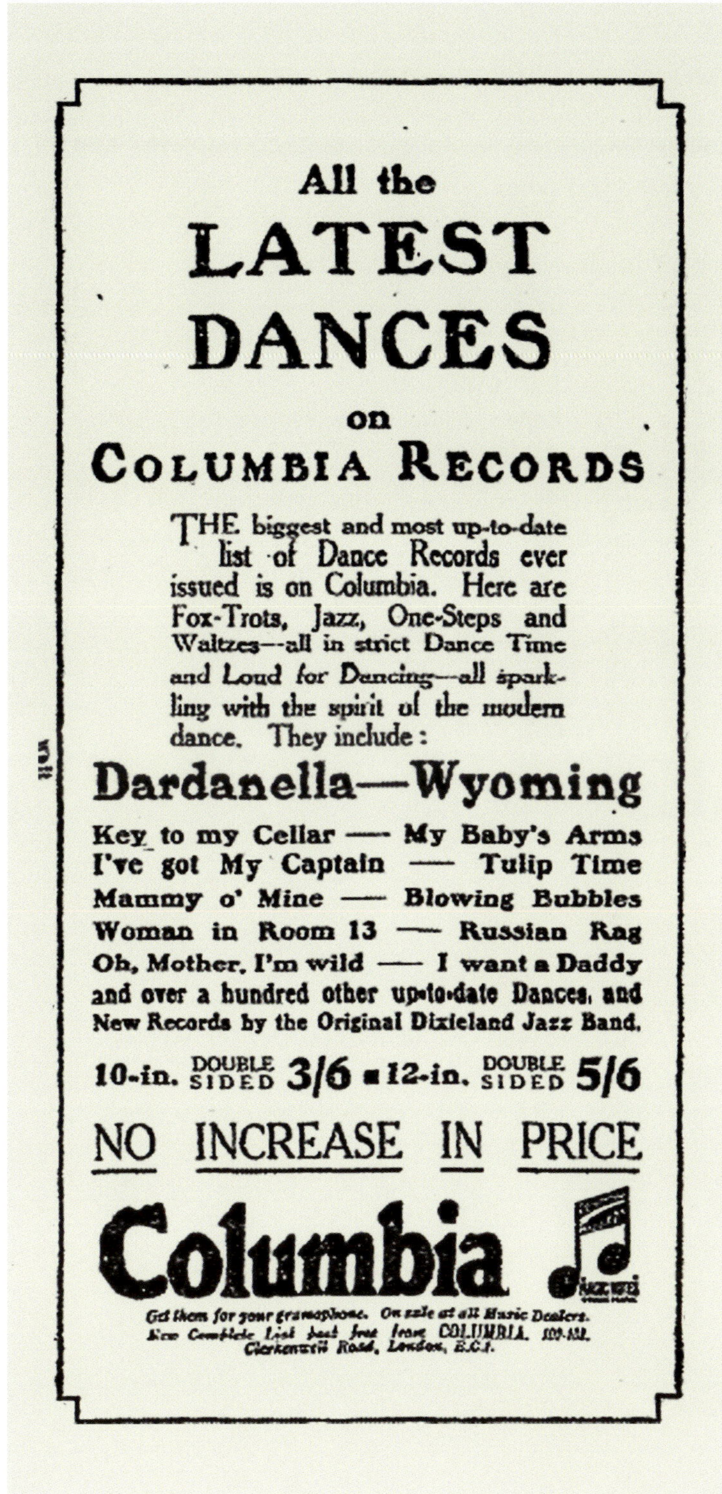

1930 Lionel Hampton his records first vibraphone solo. Whiteman band appears in film *King Of Jazz*.

1931 Ellington records "Creole Rhapsody," the first extended jazz piece.

1932 Louis Armstrong plays in London.

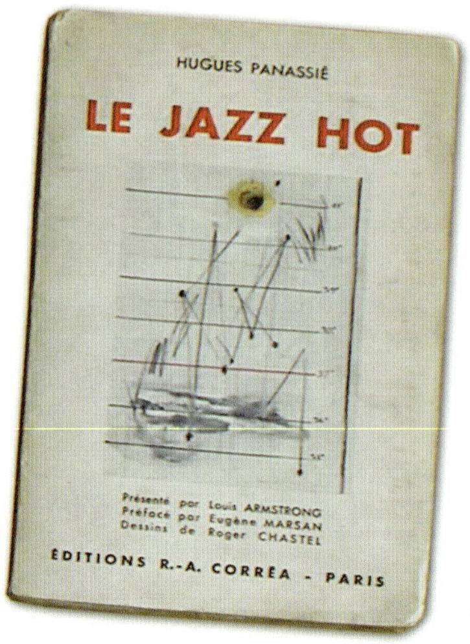

1933 Ellington band begin first their European tour.
Billie Holiday's first record (with Benny Goodman Orchestra).
Hot Club of France give their first concert.

1934 Hugues Panassie publishes *Le Jazz Hot*.
Chick Webb's band record "Stompin' At The Savoy."
Down Beat magazine launched.
Jimmie Lunceford replaces Cab Calloway at the Cotton Club.

1935 Ella Fitzgerald begins recording with Chick Webb Orchestra.
Billie Holiday begins recording with Teddy Wilson Orchestra.
Tommy Dorsey Orchestra records for Victor.

1936 Nat King Cole records with the Solid Swingers.
Benny Carter joins Henry Hall's BBC Orchestra as arranger.
Henry Hall's band travels on maiden voyage of *S.S. Queen Mary*.

1937 Billie Holiday works with Count Basie band and his band records "One O'Clock Jump."

1938 Benny Goodman performs at Carnegie Hall.
Carnegie Hall concert *From Spirituals To Swing* produced by John Hammond.
Fats Waller British tour.

1939 Glenn Miller band performs at Glen Island Casino; the band record "Moonlight Serenade" and "In The Mood."
Billie Holiday records "Strange Fruit."
Frank Sinatra records with Harry James Orchestra.
Benny Goodman hires guitarist Charlie Christian.

1940 Dizzy Gillespie and Charlie Parker trying new sounds.

1941 Bop begins in New York City.
HMV recorded Britain's "first public jazz session."

1942 "Flyin' Home" by Lionel Hampton with Illinois Jacquet a huge hit.

1943 American Forces Radio begins European broadcasts helps spread the jazz word.

1944 The first Jazz at the Philharmonic concert.

1945 Be-bop begins with Parker and Gillespie and a young Miles Davis .

1946 Swing bands starting to break up.

1947 Thelonious Monk's seminal Blue Note recordings.

1948 Birdland opens in New York.
The LP is introduced by Columbia.

1949 Trad more popular in Europe than bop.
Miles Davis records first "cool" jazz records.

1950 Ellington tours Europe.

1951 45-rpm records introduced.
First American Jazz Festival.

1954 First Newport Jazz Festival.

1955 Jimmy Smith plays jazz on the Hammond B-3 organ.

1957 Thelonious Monk is finally understood.

1958 Bill Evans joins up with Miles Davis.

1959 Miles Davis's *Kind of Blue* released.
Dave Brubeck's *Time Out* released.

1960 Free jazz and modal jazz take hold.

1962 The boom in Latin jazz begins.

1964 John Coltrane's *A Love Supreme* released.

1966 Duke Ellington Grammy lifetime achievement award.

1969 Jazz rock with Zappa, Tony Williams is brewing.

1970 Miles Davis's *Bitches Brew* released.

1971 Louis Armstrong dies.

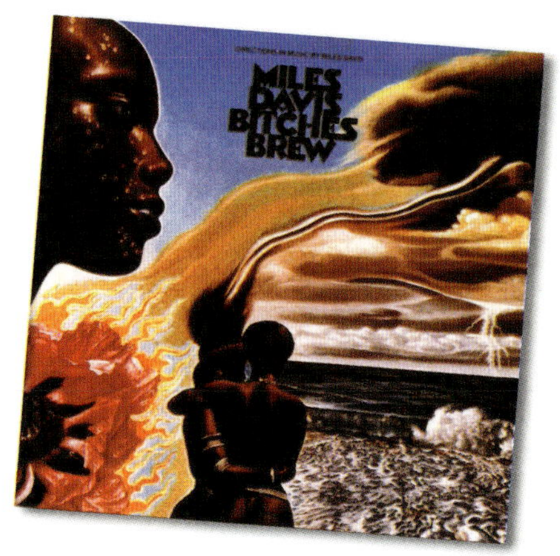

Of course the timeline of jazz doesn't end with the death of Satchmo, but while the availability of recordings on CD drives the industry onwards, the events of note increasingly concern the passing of the greats. While new musicians arrive on the scene, the opportunities for new and exciting developments are less and less… LONG LIVE JAZZ!

LOUIS ARMSTRONG

"An artist of Flaubertian purity and a character of exceptional warmth and goodness." *~ Philip Larkin*

Most people under sixty when, and even if, they think of Louis Armstrong recall a man who sang "It's A Wonderful World" or "Hello Dolly." Their recognition of his voice is from the soundtracks to films or the backing tracks to TV commercials. What many of them probably don't know is that he was a remarkable musician whose technical expertise, the genius of his musical imagination, and his dominance of the genre, made him the model for virtually every jazz musicians from the late 1920s to the outbreak of World War Two – and beyond.

Born in a slum, the son of a laborer and a part-time prostitute, Armstrong believed throughout his life that he had arrived in the world on July 4 1900; it was only after his death that his real age was discovered on church baptismal records – it was 1901. He spent his early years with his grandmother before rejoining his mother in Storyville, the area of brothels and honky tonks in New Orleans.

Armstrong's first musical foray was singing in a quartet with some other kids from around Perdido Street. They roamed Storyville singing for small change, which besides earning him a few cents also helped to train his "ear." In his early teens he was sent to the "Home for Colored Waifs," having been charged with "firing arms within the city limits" during the 1913 New Year's celebration. At "the home" he joined their band, having been given a cornet to play; he may well have been disappointed, as the teenage Louis wanted to be a drummer. Released from the home, he began playing around New Orleans, which is how he came to know and befriend King Oliver, who was considered to be the best jazz cornetist in the city. The older man became a mentor to Armstrong, but like many other members of the black community, Oliver soon left and headed north for Chicago, a city where fortunes were to be made. Around 1918 Armstrong took Oliver's place in trombonist Kid Ory's Jazz Band; he also married Daisy, a prostitute, although the stormy marriage lasted but a few months.

In 1919 Louis was playing up and down the Mississippi River on the steamers with Fate Marable's Jazz-E-Saz Band. After two years he was back in New Orleans playing at the Orchard Cabaret on Burgundy Street where his friend Zutty Singleton had a small band. It was during this period that Armstrong composed a number of songs including "I Wish I Could Shimmy Like My Sister Kate," which he sold it to a publisher for $50 and it later swept

Louis Armstrong at the Aquarium, New York City, c. July 1946.

the country. In 1922 King Oliver sent his former protégé a telegram inviting him to Chicago to join his Creole Jazz Band at the Lincoln Gardens. Soon Oliver's band was making records and Armstrong was gaining a reputation around the city as a fine cornet player. He also married again, this time to the band's pianist, Lil Hardin. Shortly afterwards the couple, at the urging of the ambitious Lil, moved to New York. Settling in the city in 1924 Louis joined Fletcher Henderson's Band, which had the reputation of being the premier black orchestra. They played "soft sweet and perfect, not the sloppy New Orleans hokum, but peppy blue syncopation."

"If anybody was Mr. Jazz it was Louis Armstrong. He was the epitome of jazz and always will be. He is what I call an American standard, an American original."
~ Duke Ellington

Armstrong's first recordings with his new boss were in October 1924, the band also included saxophonist Coleman Hawkins. It was while he was in New York that Armstrong worked with some of the women blues singers, including Bessie Smith. He was beginning to gain recognition as one of the premier players of the new "hot" music.

In November 1925 Louis returned to Chicago and rejoined his wife who had moved back earlier to start Lil's Dreamland Syncopators, they began advertising the fact that they would feature the "World's Greatest Cornetist." He also began working with his own band, which he called the Savoy Ballroom Five, but for their recordings for Okeh were simply billed as "The Hot Five." The sixty recordings he made with this wonderful band transformed jazz, inspiring players and enthusing fans in equal measure. The musicians that made up the band were Kid Ory, clarinetist, Johnny Dodds, Johnny St. Cyr on banjo and Lil on piano and vocals. The initial set of recordings by the Hot Five were very much in the New Orleans style, but as the series progressed Louis become more the featured soloist; he also did his first scat singing on the song "Heebie Jeebies." The overriding atmosphere on these recordings was one of good times, which at

Jack Teagarden, Dick Carey, Louis Armstrong, Bobby Hackett, Peanuts Hucko, Bob Haggart, and Sid Catlett, Town Hall, New York, c. July 1947.

Esquire Winner
'44 and '45
Big Sid

times masked the fact that Armstrong was still growing as a musician.

Away from the recording studio Louis was working with Carrol Dickerson's Orchestra at the Sunset Café in Chicago; among those in the band was Earl Hines who was "spanking the ivories." Early in 1927 Dickerson left and Armstrong took over the band and helped to create a battle of the bands on Chicago's 35th Street, There was King Oliver's Plantation Syncopators occupying the band stand in a club on the opposite corner of the street, while Jimmy Noone's small band at the Nest was just a few yards away. Not content with playing at the Sunset from late in the night until the early morning, Armstrong was also playing at the Vendome in the late afternoon and early evening.

In 1927 Armstrong's band became the Hot Seven on record with the addition of drummer Baby Dodds, Pete Briggs on the brass bass, with John Thomas replacing Ory. It was another step along the path of Armstrong moving away from ensemble playing to solo performances. "Potato Head Blues" is generally considered to be the best of this second group of recordings. It was during these recordings that Armstrong switched from the cornet to the trumpet. At the end of the year the band was back to its five member format, and although they only cut nine sides, these are considered to be amongst the very best of his recorded output, especially "Hotter Than That," which has been called "the most exuberant recorded performance in jazz." Intriguingly, at the same time they were performing as the Hot Six on 47th Street, at a club that Armstrong himself was running. They named it the Usonia and among the band was Hines and Armstrong's old drummer friend Zutty Singleton, who had not long arrived from New Orleans. Louis was a much better musician than businessman because the Usonia soon folded due to lack of patrons.

In 1928 the personnel of the Hot Five recordings changed to included Earl Hines on piano, whose playing can be heard on the beautiful, melancholic "West End Blues," which is arguably Armstrong's greatest recording. Louis was also seeing some fat pay packets as the Savoy Ballroom, where he was being paid $200 a week to keep him from rejoining Fletcher Henderson's band that had arrived in town. By the end of the year the Five had

"Never play a thing the same way twice." *~ Louis Armstrong*

"Of course Pops toms, but he toms from the heart."
~ Billie Holiday

become the Louis Armstrong Orchestra, although for the most part there were still five of them. Other classic recordings from this period include "Weather Bird" with a fine solo, and the ubiquitous "Basin Street Blues."

In the spring of 1929 the Chicago engagement came to an end and so Armstrong and his band headed east and played a very successful stint at the Savoy Ballroom in Harlem. He also carried on recording with his own band and played a short stint with Fletcher Henderson in the pit orchestra for the off-Broadway opening of the musical *Great Day*. He appeared in the revue *Hot Chocolates*, written by Andy Razaf and Fats Waller, and had something of a hit with their song "Ain't Misbehavin'." The song is more than a nod to the Louis Armstrong that the baby-boomer generation has come to know and love. From this point on, Louis increasingly became the "popular entertainer" rather than an out-and-out jazz musician. He, like many of his contemporaries, had to adapt their style, as they became victims, like everyone else, of the effects of the Great Depression. The one thing that Louis Armstrong had, that others didn't, was a big personality which incorporated his wider than wide grin and an almost overly expressive face. It was this that caused some to accuse him of selling out to a White audience who exploited his "Uncle Tom" approach to entertainment. It was a situation that Billie Holiday later explained away with her own unique take on the situation. "Of course Pops toms, but he toms from the heart."

"The World's Greatest Trumpeter."
~ The program at the Glasgow Empire, August 1932

JERGENS LOTION
MURRAY'S

"Armstrong is to music what Einstein is to physics and the Wright Brothers are to travel." ~ *Ken Burns' jazz documentary*

Under the guidance of his manager, the tough-talking well-connected, Joe Glaser, he begun seeking out more conventional entertainment and, by 1930, he appeared in the first of over fifty feature films. After playing with his band in Los Angeles, they worked their way back across the country. At the same time his marriage to Lil ended and he was showing signs of the strain of working so hard. Nevertheless, by 1932 Armstrong had the first of his No.1 records in America, "All of Me" from the film *Careless Lady*. He also travelled across the Atlantic to appear at the London Palladium in July, followed by other British theaters. He appeared with British musicians in concert, as well as on the radio when his London Palladium concert was broadcast live on the BBC.

The following year he was back in Britain, this time with his Harlem Hot Rhythm Band; these performances sealed Armstrong's reputation in Europe and were to be the first of many visits.

It was in 1932 that Louis gained the nickname "Satchmo," having been known as "satchelmouth" for some years. Percy Brookes, the editor of the British music newspaper, *The Melody Maker* greeted Armstrong when he arrived in Britain in 1932 with, "Hello Satchmo." It's certainly stuck, although his fellow musicians usually referred to Armstrong as "Pops."

Back in America, Armstrong's reputation as a nationwide star was enhanced by his many hit recordings prior to the end of 1935, which included "Sweethearts on Parade," "I'm in the Mood For Love," and 'You Are My Lucky Star." Armstrong had taken over Luis Russell's orchestra, which, with many personal changes, was the one he led for over a decade. Recordings such as the big band version of "Struttin' With Some Barbeque" that was first recorded with his Hot Five, showed that while his playing style may have changed, he never stopped swinging. In Armstrong's hands, mediocre material somehow became great jazz.

In 1937 he became the first black artist to have his own sponsored radio program, which enhanced his American reputation still further. He continued working with his orchestra, which took on the look and feel of a big band with a more commercial sound and sixteen musicians. Throughout the war he frequently appeared on the radio, often from US army, air force and navy bases where he entertained the service personnel. It was in 1943 that he married for the fourth and final time, settling in the Queens area of New York.

After the end of the Second World War and the

Louis Armstrong backstage at Carnegie Hall, New York City, 1947.

gradual movement away from the big band sound, Louis opted to return to the small group format; it was named the All Stars. This was a more jazz-orientated group and won him a whole new generation of fans. Initially the band really was a group of "all-stars." The band pictured features Jack Teagarden, Dick Carey, Bobby Hackett, Peanuts Hucko, Bob Haggart and Sid Catlett along with Armstrong in July 1947, which was an early incarnation of the All Stars. Others who featured in the next few years included Earl "Fatha" Hines, Cozy Cole, Billy Kyle and Barney Bigard, but as time went on Joe Glaser begun using less well known "all stars" as he realized that Armstrong was the draw.

By the mid- to late-1950s Armstrong was one of the most well known entertainers in the world. This was helped by appearances in an increasing number of films, which included *High Society* starring Bing Crosby, Frank Sinatra and Grace Kelly. What seemed like an almost non-stop round of tours saw him gain a new nickname – "Ambassador Satch." In Italy in 1959 he suffered a heart attack, from which point his health began to deteriorate, but not his enthusiasm for playing and performing. Although his performances were normally fairly predictable by this time, every now and then he surprised his audiences and especially his band by turning back the clock with some exuberant trumpet playing.

In 1964 he recorded his biggest selling record, the irrepressibly upbeat "Hello Dolly," which is far from jazz but is still a burst of unadulterated happiness. Four years later, his recording of "What A Wonderful World" topped the charts in Britain, and in the process he became the oldest performer ever to achieve such a feat.

Towards the end of his life, Louis Armstrong said, "I never tried to prove nothing, I just wanted to give a good show." He died in 1971, and his worldwide fame and the affection in which he was held wherever he went, meant that it produced headlines everywhere. Perhaps it was the U.S. State Department who summed up his passing and his contribution best of all. "His memory will be enshrined

"You can't play anything on a horn that Louis hasn't played." ~ Miles Davis

in the archives of effective international communications. The Department of State, for which he traveled on tours to almost every corner of the globe, mourns the passing of this great American."

As well as being synonymous with jazz, for a huge swathe of the American public, and similarly around the world, Armstrong was recognized by the media for his contribution to music and to entertainment in general. His photograph was featured on the covers of both *Time* and *Life* magazines, while *Variety* named him one of the "Top 100 Entertainers" of the 20th century; *Time* honored him as one of the 100 most influential people of the century. He was the first person to be honored in the *Downbeat* Jazz Hall of Fame, he is in the Rock and Roll Hall of Fame, and the ASCAP Jazz Wall of Fame. In 1972 he was posthumously honored with a Grammy Lifetime Achievement Award. Perhaps most interestingly, the city of New Orleans renamed its international airport after him.

A young reporter once asked Satchmo to define jazz, and after thinking for a moment he simply said. "Jazz is what I play for a living." Few people have earned their living while giving so much to so many.

LOUIS ARMSTRONG

BORN August 4, 1901 in New Orleans, LA

DIED July 6, 1971 in New York, NY

INSTRUMENT Cornet, Trumpet, Singer

FIRST RECORDED 1923

INFLUENCES Bunk Johnson, Joe 'King' Oliver, Kid Ory, Fletcher Henderson

RECOMMENDED LISTENING

Hot Fives and Sevens (Box Set) *(1999)*

Satchmo At Symphony Hall *(1947)*

Louis Armstrong Plays W.C. Handy *(1954)*

Great Chicago Concert *(1956)*

MARY LOU WILLIAMS

"Mary Lou Williams is perpetually contemporary. Her writing and performing have always been a little ahead throughout her career. Her music retains, and maintains, a standard of quality that is timeless. She is like soul on soul." ~ *Duke Ellington*

As a jazz musician, Mary Lou Williams was not unique, but she was a close to it as makes no difference. She played piano, wrote and arranged songs, could swing with the best of them, which she frequently did when she was in Andy Kirk's Clouds of Joy, and she also led her own band. What made her special was the fact that she kept moving forwards and, while others became stuck in some musical time warp, Mary Lou pushed the boundaries of her art.

Born Mary Elfrieda Scruggs in Atlanta in 1910, her family moved to Pittsburgh when she was very young, and it was here, as a six-year-old, that she began playing the piano, largely teaching herself. She appeared as Mary Lou Burley, which was her stepfather's name, and by the time she was fifteen she was good enough to join a group led by John Williams, who became her husband soon afterwards. They played in a band together in Memphis and recorded as John Williams' Synco Jazzers in Chicago in February 1927 – Mary Lou was still only sixteen years old.

After Chicago, Kansas City ranks up there as one of the most important cities in jazz history, and one of those that helped bolster its reputation was Andy Kirk. It was his band that Mary Lou joined in 1929 as a deputy pianist and arranger, but within the year she had been promoted to fill the piano stool as the band's full-time pianist. Kirk had moved to Kansas City from Oklahoma City, which is where Mary Lou's saxophone-playing husband had become one of Kirk's Twelve Clouds of Joy as they were first known. After the band moved to Kansas City, it was Williams' skill as an arranger that did much to enhance Kirk's band's reputation. It was her delicate swinging piano style that enhanced many of the band's recordings.

One of Mary Lou's earliest arrangements for the band was in May 1930, called simply "Mary's Idea," and while there's nothing wrong with it, it doesn't really have the panache or the range that her later material has. By 1936 "Walkin' and Swingin' " demonstrated what a skilled arranger she had become, and in 1938 "Twinklin' " highlighted her gifts both as an arranger and as a pianist.

Mary Lou Williams, New York, NY, c. 1946.

Some have suggested that while Kirk stood at the door of greatness, he never quite stepped over the line. No one suggests that he wasn't great, but sometimes, it was more that the consistency wasn't there. Others have argued that he was too lenient with his band – failing to push them that little bit harder to achieve their full potential. None of these criticisms could be blamed on Mary Lou Williams, who delivered whenever she was called upon.

In April 1930 Brunswick Records got Mary Lou to Chicago to make her first solo recordings. She recorded "Night Life" and "Drag 'Em". On the record's label it was the first time that Mary had the "Lou" added to her professional name. She'd always been plain old Mary up to that point, but Jack Kapp at Brunswick thought it sounded better and it's hard to disagree.

Her skill as an arranger was increasingly being recognized by other bandleaders: Tommy Dorsey, Earl Hines and Benny Goodman all benefited from her skill. For Benny, she did "Roll 'Em," which is typical of her driving blues piano style. She also did "Camel Hop," which featured as the signature tune of the Goodman band's radio show sponsored by the cigarette manufacturer. Goodman's offers of an exclusive, permanent contract were rejected by Williams, who much preferred to freelance.

In 1942 she left Kirk's band, having also divorced John Williams. It was the beginning of a very different phase in her career, one in which she fulfilled her potential as a jazz pianist. She moved back to Pittsburgh and formed a small group that included Harold "Shorty" Baker who had joined Kirk's band as a trumpet player in 1940. The Williams/Baker band also included a young Art Blakey on drums, but it broke up after Baker was offered a stand in the Duke Ellington Orchestra. Williams and Baker were married and they travelled together with Ellington's outfit for a while, with Williams contributing some arrangements, including "Trumpets No End", a version of "Blue Skies", the Irving Berlin tune.

THE MELODY MAKER

GIRL They All COPY

Hot Records Reviewed - - - by "ROPHONE"

Mary Lou Williams creates the phrases that become clichés

It was shortly after "Trumpets No End" that Williams and Baker split up, by which time Mary Lou had already settled in New York City, having decided that life on the road was beginning to get a little "old" after nearly twenty years. This led to Mary Lou concentrating on her work as a composer and arranger. She got a regular spot at the fashionable Café Society in New York City's Greenwich Village. She also had her own radio show, *Mary Lou Williams Piano Workshop*, on WNEW which helped secure her reputation with a wider public. While she was

"If we are to make progress in modern music, or, if you prefer, jazz, we must be willing and able to open our minds to new ideas and developments."
~ Mary Lou Williams, 1947

Mary Lou Williams in her regular spot at the fashionable Café Society, Greenwich Village, New York City, NY, c. June 1947.

regularly acknowledged by her peers, she also began to encourage other, younger, jazz musicians, including Thelonious Monk, Tadd Dameron, Bud Powell, and Dizzy Gillespie. Her involvement with Gillespie extended to composing the music for "In the Land of Oo-Bla-Dee" – so that's where The Beatles got the idea. It was Milton Orent's lyrics that Joe Carroll sang on the 1949 recording.

One of Williams' most ambitious projects was her *Zodiac Suite* composed for Moe Asch's label; it would later become the Folkways label. This series of modernist sketches, which had been premiered weekly on her WNEW show, represented the twelve signs of the zodiac. As well as recording it, she played it live first in December 1945 with a small group, and then in 1946 with the 70-piece New York Philharmonic Orchestra. On a later occasion she performed it at the Newport Festival in 1957 with Dizzy Gillespie's big band. As one critic said at the time, "It should go a long way towards validating Mary Lou Williams' place in the pantheon of modern jazz greats."

She was very much a feature in the New York music scene: she and Josh White recorded her composition "Minute Man" in 1945, and Mary Lou began appearing at the Café Society Uptown, which introduced her to a more sophisticated audience than the more left-leaning regulars at the Greenwich Village establishment. William Gottlieb himself can best describe Mary Lou's pivotal position on the scene, as he was there to witness it.

"I was a friend of Mary Lou's and particularly remember when, in 1947 she had me show up at her place for an evening gathering. The turnout was small, but choice. Among the group that appeared were three disparate geniuses who were, or became, members of *Down Beat*'s Hall of Fame: Dizzy Gillespie, the trumpeter and be-bop icon; Jack Teagarden, the premier trombonist of the era; and May Lou, herself. To top it off, there were two of the most prominent boppers: pianist-arranger Tadd Dameron and pianist Hank Jones."

In 1952 Williams travelled across the Atlantic to perform in Britain for the first time. She was there to appear in the *Big Rhythm Show* with the Cab Calloway Orchestra. Such was her reception in England, and in Europe, that she ended up staying for two years, splitting her time between London and Paris. She was helped by *Melody Maker* writer Max Jones to get around some of the stringent Musicians' Union rules that were a real problem

"Her spacious Harlem apartment was a 'salon' where, especially in the 1940s, many prominent jazz people hung out, especially – though not exclusively – those musicians whose style was at the cutting edge." *~ William Gottlieb*

Jack Teagarden, Dixie Bailey, Mary Lou Williams, Tadd Dameron, Hank Jones, Dizzy Gillespie, and Milt Orent at Mary Lou Williams' apartment, New York City, NY, c. August 1947.

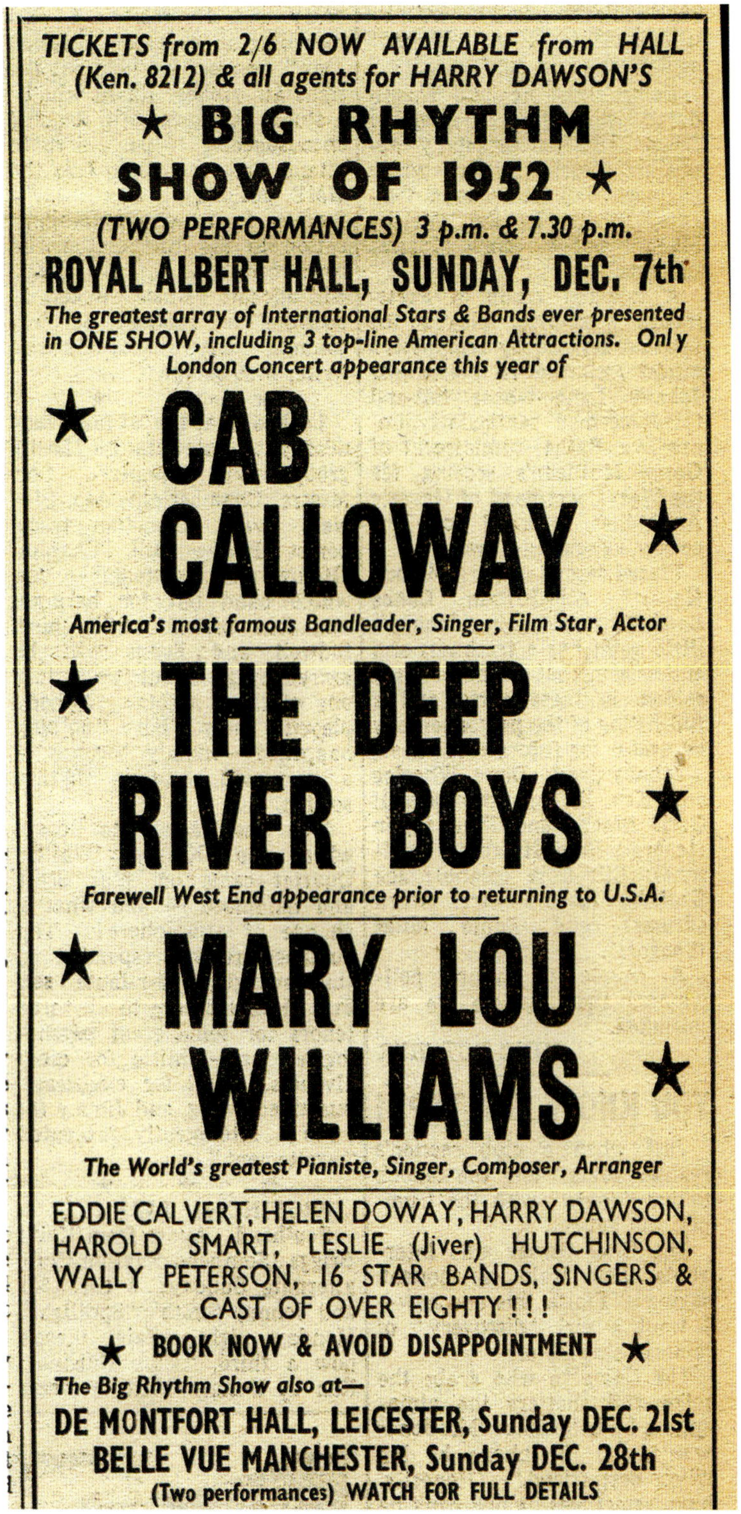

in allowing US musicians to appear in Britain; she appeared with Ted Heath and his Band at the London Palladium in 1953. By the time she moved to Paris, she had also appeared in the Netherlands and, while living in Paris, she worked with her old friend. the tenor saxophonist, Don Byas. It was like a reprise of her salon in New York, although this time it was on Paris' Left Bank and her friends included the novelist, James Baldwin, and singers, Eartha Kitt, and Annie Ross.

Her European jaunt was dogged by some money issues and while in Paris Mary Lou's state of mind proved to be somewhat fragile. It led to her discovering the Catholic faith and, as she later said, "I found God in a little garden in Paris." By late December 1954 she had resolved to return to the USA and to turn her back on performing.

After settling back in New York, Williams recovered to the point where she felt able to perform again, with the spiritual support of her new-found faith. Her first appearance was with her old friend Dizzy Gillespie at Newport, where she performed *The Zodiac Suite*. She also began working with troubled musicians, using her faith in this more practical way by creating charity shops to collect money for their welfare. She also began composing sacred works. Her first in 1962, *Black Christ of the Andes*, celebrated a seventeenth-century Dominican – the first black canonized by the Roman Catholic Church. Later, she composed several masses, including one in honor of Martin Luther King, that she had hoped to perform in the

"I'm the only living musician that has played all the eras. Other musicians lived through the eras and they never changed their styles."
~ Mary Lou Williams

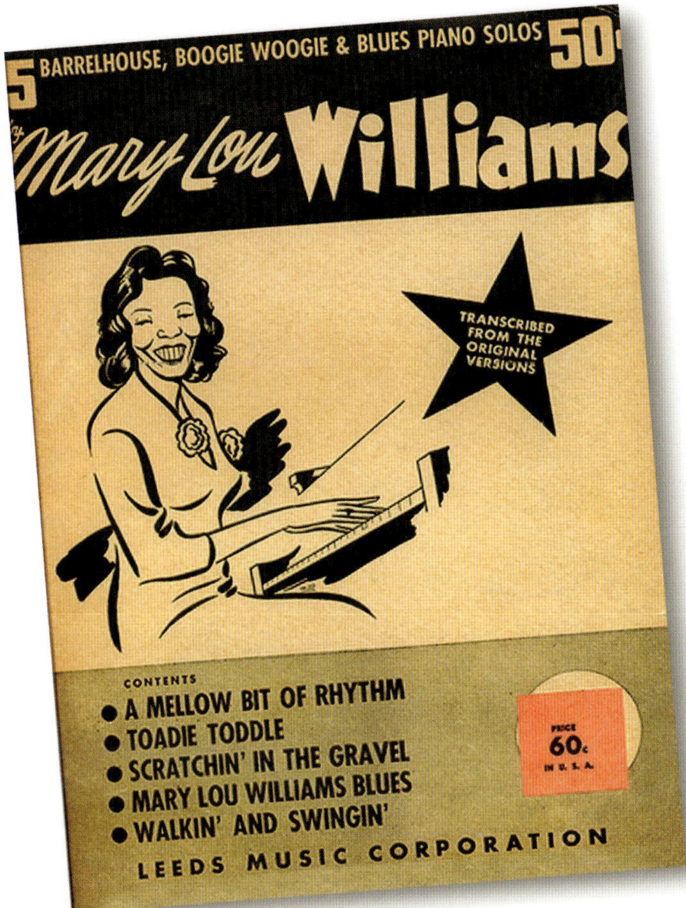

Vatican in 1969, but there were objections over the use of drums.

Williams did not turn her back on the world of jazz, and continued to perform with many old friends, as well as continuing to arrange for some of the legendary big bands, including both Duke Ellington and Count Basie. As ever, she was still at the cutting edge, working with the avant-garde pianist Cecil Taylor, and on another occasion with the Alvin Ailey Dance Theater. In 1977 Williams, approaching seventy herself, took up teaching at Duke University. In 1978 she performed at the White House in *The Salute To Jazz* concert, hosted by President Carter, where she played "Somewhere Over The Rainbow". Mary Lou Williams, a true jazz genius died in May 1981.

MARY LOU WILLIAMS

BORN May 8, 1910 in Atlanta, Georgia

DIED May 28, 1981 in Durham, North Carolina

INSTRUMENT Piano

FIRST RECORDED 1927

INFLUENCES Fats Waller, James P. Johnson

RECOMMENDED LISTENING

The Mary Lou Willaims Story *(2008)*

Zodiac Suite *(1945)*

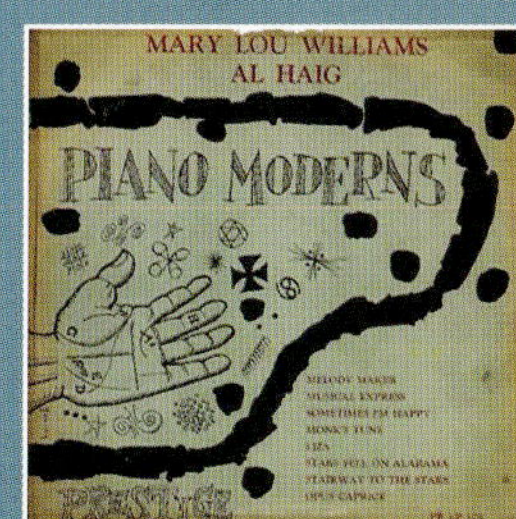

Piano Moderns *(1950)*

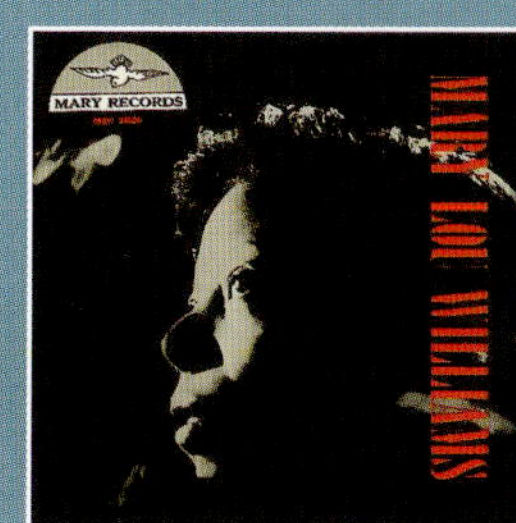

Black Christ of the Andes *(1963)*

BABY
POWDER

DUKE ELLINGTON

***"I immediately recognized that I had encountered a great creative artist – and the first American composer to catch in his music the true jazz spirit."** ~ Irving Mills*

The Duke's jazz was innovative, with arrangements that featured his piano playing against a rich, deep sound played by the brilliant musicians that he always had in his orchestra. Over five hundred of the best jazz musicians in the world passed through his ranks; rarely was anyone fired, because he hired the best. At the same time, he wrote wonderful, popular songs, extended jazz works, suites, and also gave sacred concerts. Versatility was what the Duke was all about; he was the Renaissance man of jazz.

Edward Kennedy Ellington's father was a butler in a house not far from the White House; he wanted his son to become an artist. Ellington senior expected his children to behave themselves, to dress and speak according to their upbringing, which was much better than most of young Edward's future colleagues. He began studying piano when he was seven or eight; back then ragtime was about as jazzy as things got in the capital. He learned to read music early on, which helped him to achieve greatness later.

It was when he was a teenager that he first became known as "Duke;" he was described as being somewhat detached back then, maybe even a little haughty. He made his professional debut as a teenager in 1916 having learned ragtime piano from a pianist named Doc Perry. Even before he made his debut, he had composed his first rag. He played in the capital's nightspots with a small group that included drummer Sonny Greer, who worked with the Duke for many years.

In 1922 he took his trio to New York City to work, but it was a failure. Encouraged to return the following year by Fats Waller, he took his Washingtonians to a job at Barron's in Harlem; a few months later they were uptown at the Kentucky Club on Broadway. Soon the

Duke Ellington in his dressing-room at the Paramount Theater, New York, NY, c. September 1946.

"He's the Duke of Ellington." ~ Ella Fitzgerald

Duke was working up more complicated arrangements as well as experimenting with his own material.

Not long after Duke began to find success in New York, he decided he needed a manager. Irving Mills, a music publisher and all around man about music proved to be the right choice when he secured the prestigious gig at the Cotton Club. When they opened, the band was a ten-piece having been joined by clarinetist Barney Bigard, along with saxophonists, Johnny Hodges on alto and Harry Carney on baritone.

The Washingtonians had first recorded back in November 1924 and over the next couple of years cut a few more sides. It wasn't until 1926, when Duke was being billed as Duke Ellington and his Kentucky Club Orchestra, that he really started to show promise in the studio with "A Night in Harlem" and the first rendition of "East St Louis Toodle-o"; a later version of this with "Toodle-oo" on the end made the *Billboard* best sellers list. Over the next two to three years the Ellington Orchestra was rarely out of the studio; "Creole Love Call", "Black and Tan Fantasy" and "The Mooche" all made the *Billboard* chart.

Pivotal to Duke's success were his radio broadcasts from the Cotton Club, which carried his name directly into homes all across America on the CBS network (which had been founded in 1927.) As the 1920s came to an end Ellington's orchestra were not just known in America – word had spread to Europe. In June 1931 Ellington was in a studio in Camden, New Jersey to record one of his most ambitious records – "Creole Rhapsody." It took up both sides of a 78-rpm record, something completely new for a jazz band – this is what classical orchestras did, not jazz bands. It certainly gives some insight into what Ellington was thinking and we can only speculate on what he might have done had better technology been available. He went on to create many extended works during the 1930s, the most creative period of his entire career.

Ellington eventually left the Cotton Club and began appearing in cities all over America. In 1933 he embarked upon his most ambitious tour, crossing the Atlantic to appear in Britain. The Duke's records sold in large numbers, particularly in, "London and university cities," according to the press. He appeared at the London Palladium for the first time on June 12, 1933 and was

"Competition only makes you play better." ~ Duke Ellington

"Duke Ellington was the real pioneer in jazz concerts."
~ Norman Granz

afforded a "wildly enthusiastic welcome." Among those in the audience was Nesuhi Ertegun, who had taken his younger brother Ahmet to witness "the King of Jazz" as the newspapers dubbed the Duke. Ahmet would later co-found Atlantic Records.

The 1930s saw some of the Duke's biggest selling records including, "It Don't Mean a Thing If it Ain't Got That Swing", "Sophisticated Lady", "Stormy Weather", "Cocktails for Two", "Solitude" and "Caravan." On many of these records, as well as Ellington's 1933 trip to London, were some outstanding musicians, including Barney Bigard on clarinet, Cootie Williams on trumpet and Ben Webster on tenor sax.

By the time Ellington returned to Britain in 1939, Billy

Strayhorn, Duke's longtime collaborator, had joined the band as arranger, composer, and second pianist. He added yet more depth and variety to the Ellington sound. The tours in the USA had got bigger and more lavish as the years went by. Instead of travelling by bus, like most bands, Duke Ellington's Famous Orchestra, as they were billed, travelled in their own Pullman car, although this was not the inspiration for one of the band's most famous records, "Take The A Train", which they recorded in Hollywood in January 1941. The song, written by Billy Strayhorn, which has become synonymous with the band, as well as becoming their signature tune, was actually about the New York subway.

"Take The A Train" was just one of a whole string of amazing recordings made between 1939 and 1942, when the orchestra were at their absolute best. But even these were to be eclipsed by the Duke's first really long work – "Black, Brown and Beige" – which had its premiere at Carnegie Hall in November 1943. The inspiration behind the piece was to tell the story of the African-American struggle. It was the first in a series of concerts, which showcased Ellington's longer works. While the Duke was not the first jazz musician to have played at Carnegie Hall, his was the most ambitious musical program.

With the strictures of war, followed by the decline in interest in big bands, Ellington's Orchestra was no

"Fate is being kind to me. Fate doesn't want me to be too famous too young." ~ Duke Ellington

different to almost any other in that there were fewer opportunities on both record and in concert. Fortunately, Ellington was better placed than the others in that he had his song publishing affairs well managed. It meant that the royalties from song writing were subsidizing his band to some extent. "Don't Get Around Much Anymore", "Mood Indigo" and "Sophisticated Lady" were just three of the compositions that earned significant sums, running well into six figures for each song, even during the 1940s.

By the early 1950s things had become much worse for all of the big bands. Ellington, in particular, suffered when he lost two of his stalwarts – Johnny Hodges and Sonny Greer – and for a while it seemed that the Duke might actually fold his touring band altogether. However, the advent of the long-playing record allowed Duke to focus his composing efforts on increasingly interesting pieces. At the same time there were also foreign tours, but things certainly weren't what they used to be.

Then in 1956 there was something of a revival in the Orchestra's fortunes, beginning with an appearance at the Newport Jazz Festival in July. With new saxophonist, Paul Gonsalves, playing a six-minute solo on "Diminuendo and Crescendo in Blue", a piece dating from the late thirties, the Ellington Orchestra took the festival by storm. They were helped, too, by the return to the fold of Johnny Hodges and a new record deal with Columbia Records, releasing the highly successful *Ellington at Newport*. On the

The Duke and his Orchestra.

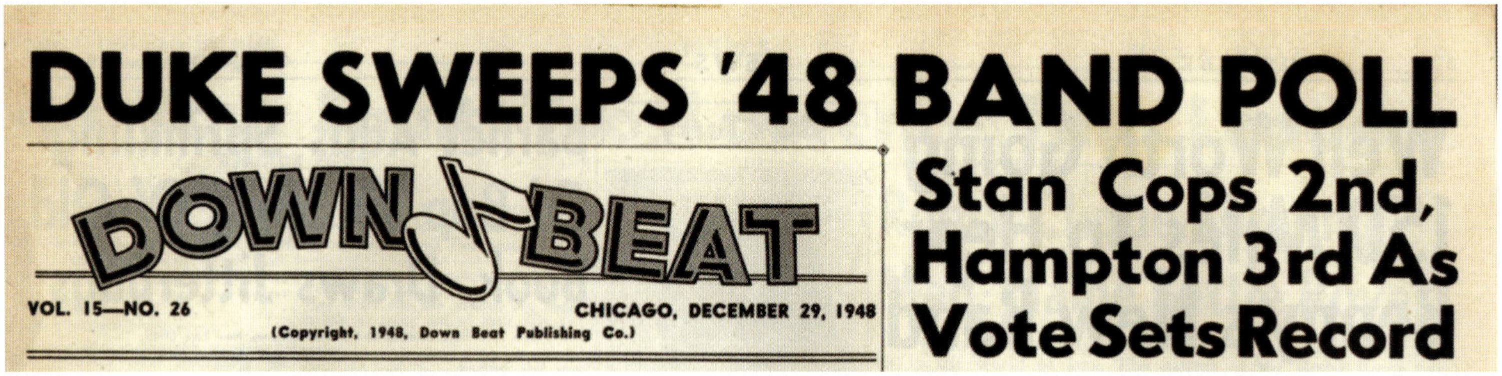
DUKE SWEEPS '48 BAND POLL

DOWN BEAT

VOL. 15—NO. 26 CHICAGO, DECEMBER 29, 1948

(Copyright, 1948, Down Beat Publishing Co.)

Stan Cops 2nd, Hampton 3rd As Vote Sets Record

back of this resurgence, another major European tour in 1958 gave the band a renewed international status that had been in danger of ebbing away. Ellington and Strayhorn also wrote the score for the film *Anatomy of a Murder* in 1959, which added another level of interest in what they were doing.

In the early sixties Ellington also worked with some younger jazz stars, including, Charles Mingus and John Coltrane, which helped to introduce him to a new generation of fans recently brought into the jazz fold by this new breed of musicians. But it wasn't just the new breed that were acknowledging the Duke; Ella Fitzgerald recorded her songbook tribute to Ellington – it was a master class.

In 1965 he recorded his first concert of sacred music, which met with mixed reviews, a fact that did nothing to deter the Duke from reprising it all over the world on numerous occasions. At the other end of the musical spectrum he did the music for a Frank Sinatra film called *Assault On A Queen*; the music was much better than the movie but it did not feature Sinatra singing. The following year the Ellington Orchestra worked on an album with Frank called *Francis A and Edward K*. This unique collaboration went almost unnoticed at the time of its release, failing to even make the Top 40 album chart, even though it featured THE voice alongside one of THE great jazz orchestras.

Among the songs they recorded was the beautiful "Indian Summer," with a stunning arrangement by Billy May that is both reflectively modern, and at the same time old fashioned, as befits a song written in 1919. It is one of the best songs Frank ever recorded for Reprise. Johnny Hodges' sax solo certainly adds to the overall effect and, so enthralled was Sinatra during its recording, that when Hodges finishes his solo, Sinatra is half a second late in coming in to sing. Hodges died two years later and this was a fitting elegy to a great saxophonist.

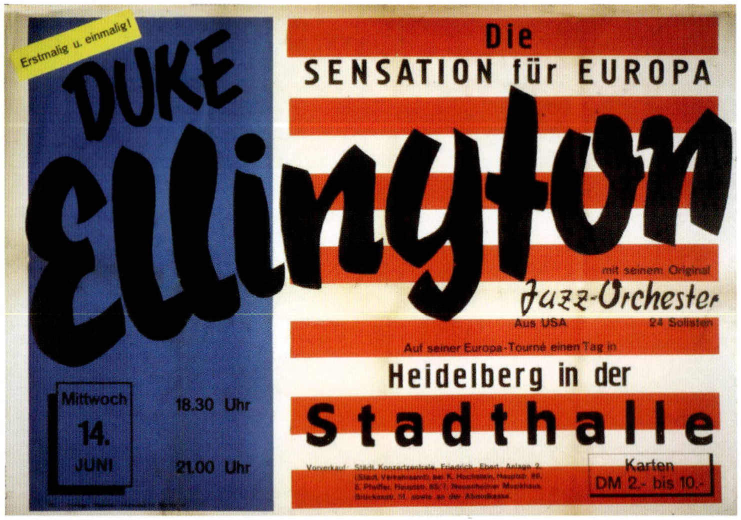

Left to right: Junior Raglin, bass; Lawrence Brown, trombone; Johnny Hodges, alto sax; Duke Ellington, Ray Nance, trumpet, and Sonny Greer, drums at the Aquarium, New York, NY, c. November 1946.

DUKE ELLINGTON

BORN April 29, 1899 in Washington DC

DIED May 24, 1974 in New York, NY

INSTRUMENT Pianist, Composer, Bandleader

FIRST RECORDED 1924

INFLUENCES Doc Perry, James P. Johnson, Fats Waller

RECOMMENDED LISTENING

Ellington At Newport
Columbia, 1956

The Great Paris Concert
Atlantic, 1963

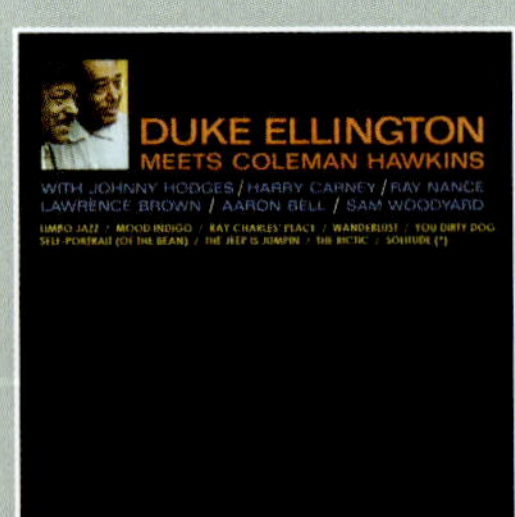

Duke Ellington Meets Coleman Hawkins *(1962)*

... And His Mother Called Him Bill *(1967)*

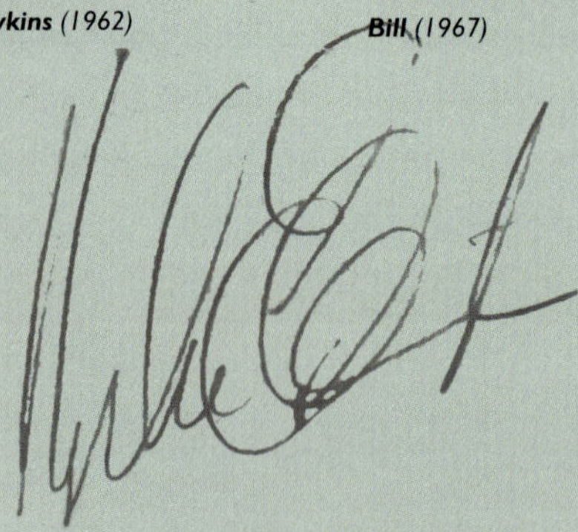

In 1969 Ellington received the Medal of Freedom at the White House; it would certainly have shocked his father, but possibly not. By the 1970s Ellington was working all around the world. This included a tour of Russia in 1971 and a concert in Westminster Abbey in London in December 1973 that featured his sacred music. The Duke was suffering from lung cancer by this time, and he died on May 25, 1974.

Unquestionably, Duke Ellington was one of the greatest composers of the twentieth century. He sold records in large quantities and created a sound that was all his own, for which jazz will forever be the richer.

Coleman Hawkins

"As far as I'm concerned, I think Coleman Hawkins was the President first, right? As far as myself, I think I'm the second one." *~ Lester Young*

The "Dean of Saxophonists" or the "Hawk," as his many fans around the world knew him, did more than any other musician to establish the tenor sax. The suave and sophisticated player was a long way from what many people imagine a jazz musician to be like, although his love of drinking ensured that he lived up to that particular cliché. He was a powerful, passionate and always original tenor player. "Bean", as others called him, lived in London and toured Europe extensively for five years during the 1930s, which did a great deal to spread the jazz word.

Coleman Randolph Hawkins, born in 1904, hailed from St. Joseph, Missouri, the town where the Pony Express began its route west. His mother, whose maiden name was Coleman, played piano and organ in her local church and so it was from her that the man who became known as "Hawk" had his musical grounding. He had his first lessons at five years old, and would later (somewhat mysteriously, some have suggested) say he was able to read music before he could read words. Later on, he played the cello and later still, he picked up a saxophone; by the age of twelve he was good enough to be offered a job playing with a local band.

His parents were not poor, having the money to send him to boarding school where he was encouraged to continue with the cello, but not allowed to play the sax. During holidays back home he continued to play with local bands. On leaving school, the eighteen-year-old Hawkins became one of Mamie Smith's Original Jazz Hounds, playing on the road as part of her touring show.

Mamie Smith had made history in 1920 by releasing "Crazy Blues," which is generally regarded as the first blues song to be recorded. Smith was not specifically a blues singer, but more a vaudeville and cabaret singer; then again at this time there was no such thing as a blues-only singer. By the time young Coleman joined her band, she was almost forty years old. Soon after Hawkins joined they played The Garden of Joy in New York and before long he was in the studio with Mamie recording four sides in May 1922. By early 1923 he had left the band, having decided to settle in New York to find work wherever he could. He must have been confident of finding it because he had been earning $50 a week with the Jazz Hounds, with featured billing as "The Saxophone Boy."

In August 1923 he was back in the studio working with Fletcher Henderson's orchestra. It was the start of a long-running relationship in which Hawkins appeared on

numerous Henderson recordings. He was there in October 1924 when Louis Armstrong played with Henderson on his first recording with what was the premier black orchestra of the day. Armstrong had joined the band during their residency at the Roseland Ballroom and there was apparently some antipathy between the two jazzmen. Hawkins, a man of sophisticated taste, may well have taken a good deal of enjoyment from Armstrong's less sophisticated ways.

Others in the Henderson band found Coleman less than amusing, and in truth more of an annoyance. While musically his timekeeping was impeccable, his inability to turn up anywhere promptly for anything else was legendary. Likewise, his capacity for drink without any effect caused some amazement.

The Henderson gig was not Hawkins' only work. Among those he recorded with were Bessie Brown, the Chocolate Dandies along with Fats Waller, and McKinney's Cotton Pickers. He also played live with a

"He put a lot of beauty into his playing; he was full of music." *~ Drummer Eddie Locke*

whole host of musicians around New York City, enabling him to live with his wife, a former dancer with Mamie Smith's show, in one of the best houses in Harlem. Hawkins' main source of work remained the Henderson Orchestra, both recordings and in the ballrooms that included the Roseland and the Savoy, as well as others throughout the east and south of the country.

In April 1933 Hawkins got involved in an unusual session in New York, playing with Spike Hughes and his Negro Orchestra. Spike was an Englishman who had decided to go to New York to record with authentic jazz

"I'm a classics man, but then I started like that." *~ Coleman Hawkins*

musicians, as he saw them, rather than the his fellow countrymen with whom he had been working with for the last three years. Besides Hawkins, there was Benny Carter and Sid Catlett among the group of very good musicians that Hughes worked with. So good did Hughes think these recordings, that he virtually gave up jazz from then on as he thought he had achieved all he ever could.

In September 1933 Coleman finally went into the studio with his own orchestra for the very first time to record three sides, including the lovely "Heartbreak Blues". In March the following year he was back with his orchestra to record three more, including "I Ain't Got Nobody" and "On The Sunny Side of The Street". Somewhat unusually for an American musician at this time, his next recording date was to be in London in November. Henderson's band had been due to tour in England, but it fell through, leading Hawkins to make contact with British bandleader Jack Hylton to arrange a visit by himself.

Hawkins wasted no time getting to London because he appeared at the London palladium from April 16, 1934 with a Jack Hylton Orchestra show called *In Town Tonight*. After London it went on the road, appearing in theatres that included the famous Glasgow Empire where they received some great reviews. The Hawk was being billed

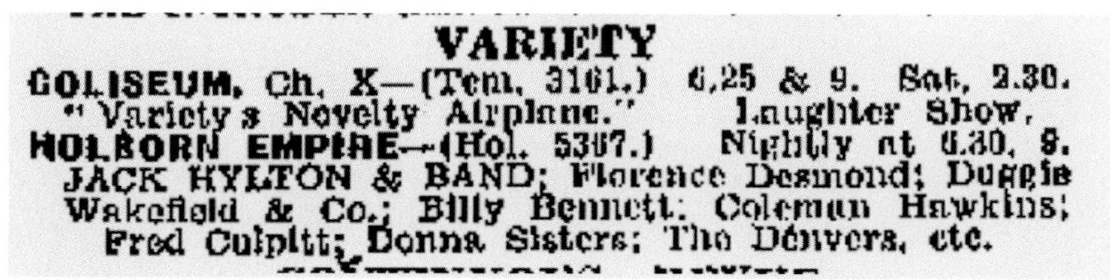
VARIETY
COLISEUM, Ch. X—(Tem. 3161.) 6.25 & 9. Sat. 2.30.
"Variety's Novelty Airplane." Laughter Show.
HOLBORN EMPIRE—(Hol. 5367.) Nightly at 6.30, 9.
JACK HYLTON & BAND; Florence Desmond; Duggie Wakefield & Co.; Billy Bennett; Coleman Hawkins; Fred Culpitt; Donna Sisters; The Denvers, etc.

Coleman Hawkins at the Spotlite Club, New York, c. September 1946.

"King Coleman Hawkins described as the world's greatest saxophonist, is another outstanding item." ~ The Scotsman, *August 14, 1934*

as "King Coleman Hawkins."

At the November session Hawkins recorded the excellent "Lady Be Good" and the aptly entitled "Lost in A Fog," which features a beautiful solo by the Hawk. The British musicians included Stanley Black, a young pianist who would later work in film and classical music.

The trip away was supposed to be a short, but Henderson kept extending his stay, as well as travelling to the Continent to play and record in Paris, Zurich, and Amsterdam; he also performed in Denmark and Belgium, but kept a flat in London as his base. In Paris he recorded an inspired rendition of "Crazy Rhythm" with Stéphane Grappelly and Django Reinhardt. One of his last European appearances was with Jack Hylton in London at the Holborn Empire in May 1939.

With war looming, the Hawk headed home and got an orchestra together to begin a residency at Kelly's Stable, a New York club. On October 11 he was back in the recording studio, cutting four sides. Among them was the sublime "Body and Soul", which just about everyone at the time as well as since have agreed is as close to perfection as it's possible to get. It was one hell of a way to put every other aspiring tenor sax player on notice that he was back.

His manager picked up from where Hawkins had left things in Britain by billing him as the "World's Greatest Saxophone Player." In this guise he fronted a big band that played the Savoy Ballroom and the Apollo Theater in Harlem, among other venues, but it was not the way to present Hawkins or his music as he had none of the showman qualities that were needed to pull off live

"Coleman often comes into buy recordings of symphony and chamber music, sometimes opera, but seldom jazz. " ~ *The owner of Goody's Record Shop, New York City*

Coleman Hawkins at the Spotlite Club, New York, c. September 1946.

gigs. They did manage one session in August 1940 at which they recorded four sides including "Serenade To A Sleeping Beauty" which, in title alone, was a hat tip towards the classical music that Hawkins increasingly listened to; musically it was standard big band fare, although of the classier variety.

By 1941 he was back working with a small group and feeling much more comfortable as they played in Chicago as well as dates around the Midwest. By the end of the war he was mainly working in California; he even appeared in a film, *The Crimson Canary*, with trumpeter, Howard McGhee and bassist, Oscar Pettiford. He also appeared on the Jazz Philharmonic tour in 1946, which was the first of many that he undertook; on the later tours he appeared with trumpeter Roy Eldridge who was also his good friend. In the late 1940s he once again returned to Europe for the first of a number of tours that stretched well into the 1950s.

"For the guitar, there is Segovia; for the cello, Casals; and for the tenor saxophone, there was Coleman Hawkins."
~ The Hawk's obituary

One role that the Hawk embraced with some relish was as one of jazz's elder statesmen. He was quick to tell people about Miles Davis before almost anyone was aware of him. In 1944 he also worked with some of the rising stars, including Dizzy Gillespie and Max Roach where they played some of the earliest bebop recordings. His role as a father figure extended to opening his apartment, which overlooked New York's Central Park, to up

Coleman Hawkins and Miles Davis at the Three Deuces, New York, c. July 1946.

and coming players. He loved to cook for them and you rarely heard jazz in the background – it was more likely to be Bach. In 1954 he issued his album *Jazz Tones* that is considered to be a classic. More touring, both at home and abroad, kept Coleman in front of an admiring audience.

By the early sixties things on the work front were not easy as jazz was changing; when you'd been around as long as the Hawk, there were some who just considered him old-fashioned. He did record with Duke Ellington in 1962, did an album of bossa nova around the same time, and played regularly in some of New York's best clubs, but his fervor for playing was not what it had been.

The life of a hard-drinking jazzman had begun to catch up with him. While his reputation for consuming industrial quantities of drink, especially brandy, was unrivalled, there's only so long the body can withstand such punishment. In 1967 he collapsed while on stage in Toronto. and by this point he was really an alcoholic. By the December of 1967 he was appearing one last time in Britain at Ronnie Scott's club. He told critic Max Jones that he was looking forward to returning to the UK more regularly. Sadly, it was to be his last visit and one of his last appearances. He did play once more in Chicago in April 1969, but a month later he died.

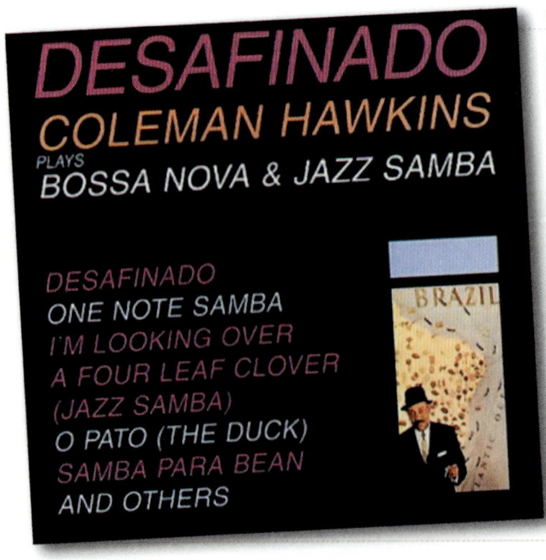

COLEMAN HAWKINS

BORN November 21, 1904 in St. Joseph, Missouri

DIED May 19, 1969 in New York, NY

INSTRUMENT Tenor Sax

FIRST RECORDED 1944

INFLUENCES Louis Armstrong, Bach, Shostakovich

RECOMMENDED LISTENING

Jazz Tones *(1954)*

The Hawk Flies High *(1957)*

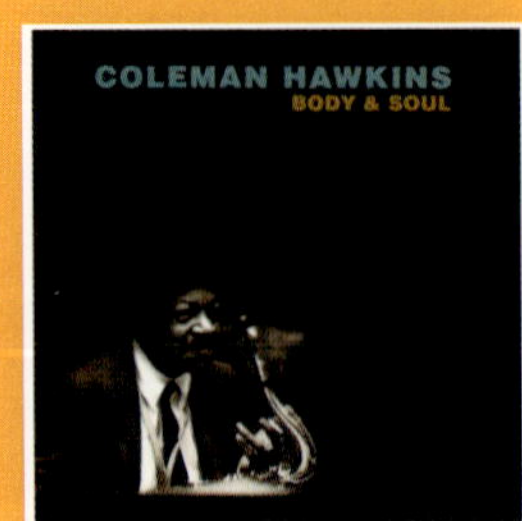

Body & Soul *(1996)*

Coleman Hawkins Encounters Ben Webster *(1997)*

In A Mellow Tone *(1960)*

Count Basie

"The band's business, as Basie saw it, was to provide swinging dance music." ~ Ted Williams

Whether it was back in the 1930s with the limited technology that was available to record the sound, or many years later, when Count Basie worked extensively with Frank Sinatra during the 1960s, and they were captured in glorious hi-fi, the Basie band always sounded "large, robust and always swinging." But perhaps most surprising of all, was that the Basie band always sounded so fresh.

William Basie was born in Red Bank, New Jersey on August 21, 1904 and took piano lessons at a young age. Initially he thought about becoming a drummer, but fortunately the piano won him over and soon he was watching the piano greats – Willie "The Lion" Smith, James P. Johnson, and Fats Waller. Taking what he saw and applying it to his own playing, he started out as a stride pianist, which takes its name from the way the pianist's left hand "strides" up and down the keyboard.

Basie began his career playing in various touring bands, and ended up in Kansas City in 1927, where he decided to settle. He was a member of Walter Page's Blue Devils, recording two sides in November of the following year. He was also playing with Bennie Moten's Orchestra and it was with them that Bill Basie first recorded, a month before the Walter Page session. Basie stayed with Moten until 1935, when the bandleader died following some complications after an operation on his tonsils.

Striking out on his own, he formed a nine-piece band that he named, The Barons of Rhythm, and among its members was the brilliant saxophonist Lester Young. The following year he recorded as the Count Basie Blues Five, with Jimmy Rushing on vocals, before he finally settled on Count Basie and his Orchestra in January 1937. It was probably shortly before this, while the band had been broadcasting on radio, that the announcer called Basie "Count" and the name stuck.

Walter Page was in the band, along with Lester Young, Buck Clayton and Jimmy Rushing. The first sides the Basie Band cut were in January of 1937, included "Honeysuckle Rose" and the fabulous "Roseland Shuffle," which showcased the Count's piano style. They had been working the Roseland Ballroom, so it was by way of homage. While still retaining elements of the stride style with which he had grown up, he was now playing with fewer notes that gave the arrangements more "air" and created what would become his trademark style.

By 1937 Basie had headquartered himself in New York, having signed for Decca Records, who were anxious to get their new signing into the studio to record a number of new sides. Basie had already been in the studio before recording for Decca, to do four sides under the

*"**Sometimes we can't wait to get on the stand, and we hate to quit when the night is over.**" ~ Ernie Williams, Basie arranger and band member*

pseudonym Jones Smith Incorporated as he had already signed for the label. This included the wonderful "Oh Lady Be Good," which features Lester Young on his first session.

Two months after the first Decca session, they were back in the studio and with them for the first time was a guitarist whose playing of chords across the beat would do much to make them swing and help define what we know as the Basie sound. His name was Freddie Green, and over thirty years later, he was still there doing his very particular thing. Green was just one of many sidemen who made the Basie band the epitome of a swinging jazz ensemble.

For the band's session in July 1937 Basie came up with a new tune, "One O'clock Jump," which became a hit and the band's theme for many years. Over the years, Count Basie revisited his tune on numerous occasions, reinventing it, and making it one of the most well-known pieces in big band jazz. For a while in 1937, the Basie band also worked with Billie Holiday: there are a couple of songs that were recorded at the Savoy Ballroom in New York City, one of which was the beautiful "They Can't Take Away From Me." A booking at the Famous Door club in New York helped gain New York's approval of the band, which had been a little slow in coming. A string of radio broadcasts that were heard coast to coast did the trick for the rest of America, and for the next decade the band was one of the most popular in the nation.

By the time the Basie band was at the Famous Door, Helen Humes had become the singer and she did a great job on songs that included "And the Angels Sing" that received a lot of air play. While the band changed personnel to continually improve its sound, it did maintain the key members for longer periods than most. It was certainly a band that seemed to enjoy being together as much as they enjoyed playing together. Basie must take credit for this, in that he was a good leader and gave his band the environment in which to flourish as musicians, as well as to have fun doing it. Basie's love of humor was well known, but as many have commented over the years, he was also a gentleman.

Key to the success and the sound of the band was the Basie rhythm section. Besides Basie's light and airy piano and Freddie Green's guitar, there was Walter Page's bass and the sensitive drumming of Jo Jones. Basie regularly referred to Jones as the "boss" the head man in the band – he had a point, but he was being his humble self. Perhaps it was the rhythm section that made the band so accessible to listeners.

*"**Count was my favourite big-band leader. I can't say one bad thing about him.**" ~ Trombonist Dickie Wells, who played with Basie for ten years*

Count Basie at the Aquarium, New York, between 1946 and 1948.

"I've waited twenty years for this moment." ~ Frank Sinatra walking into United Recorders on October 2, 1962 to begin work with Count Basie.

There's no doubt that the Basie band made jazz "listenable" to people who perhaps didn't realize they liked jazz. But although they were very much a jazz band, they were also a band that played emotional music, which was simple yet stylish.

Throughout the forties, the Basie band remained popular on record and on radio, but by 1950 things in the band business were not good and Basie called it a day. For two years he had an eight-piece band, but then in 1952 he resurrected his orchestra, unofficially calling it the New Testament band. Throughout the 1950s Basie came up with a string of great albums, including *The Atomic Mr. Basie*, *April in Paris*, *The Count Basie Dance Session*. At the same time his live appearances thrilled many, and not just in America. He became, along with Armstrong and Ellington, one of the few jazz players to gain a wide-ranging level of recognition around the world. In 1957 Basie played London's prestigious Royal Festival Hall and wowed British audiences on a tour that took in Sheffield and Bradford. He was so good at the Royal Festival Hall that Princess Margaret, who went to see his 6.00pm show, went back to see him again at 9.00pm.

The Basie band's secret weapon during the 1950s was Neil Hefti who did most of the arrangements. He had played trumpet for Woody Herman's band and later on he worked with Sinatra. He had his own band and also composed "The Batman Theme." As Miles Davis said, "If

Count Basie on piano, Ray Bauduc on drums at the Howard Theater, Washington, DC, c. 1941.

it weren't for Neal Hefti, the Basie band wouldn't sound as good as it does. But Neal's band can't play those same arrangements nearly as well." That said a lot about Basie, who always tried to surround himself with the most talented people.

By 1962 the Basie band, as well as performing and releasing albums on their own, began a relationship with Frank Sinatra that lasted for four years. In October the two legends went into the studio in Los Angeles for three days to work on a new album. Somewhat appropriately the first song they did together that day was, "Nice Work If You Can Get It," which is classic Sinatra, made perfect by Basie and a great Hefti arrangement. When the album, simply called *Sinatra – Basie* came out in early 1963 it sold better than anything the singer had done for several years. The Basie band cooks and swings like no other that Frank had previously sung with, and this was arguably the best band that Basie had ever put together. So good were the Count's boys that even Frank was put in the shade.

By June 1963 they were back in the studio working on

"I think the band can really swing when it swings easy, when it can just play along like you are cutting butter"
~ Count Basie

tracks that became *It Might as Well Be Swing*, which, while it's not as good as the original *Sinatra – Basie* album, offers up some great moments. Basie began playing some gigs with Sinatra and in November Sinatra and the Basie band were booked into the Sands in Las Vegas for a series of shows. One that the two of them were due to do, as a benefit for Martin Luther King, was cancelled as it was set for a couple of days after John F. Kennedy was shot.

The following year in June, Sinatra played the Newport Jazz Festival with the Count. Quincy Jones, like he did in Las Vegas, conducted the Basie band. The Festival's organizer George Wein had asked Basie if he could get Frank to play the festival, and he readily agreed. "The news started a gold rush matched only by teenagers in search of seats to a Beatles bash," said one paper. Some of the jazz purists were less enthusiastic, but then again they always have been. Legend has it that Sinatra only spoke to Basie once during the show to say. "Cook, cook, cook, cook, baby, cook." There were more shows in 1965, culminating in another run at the Sands in January and February 1966. This was recorded and became the double album *Frank Sinatra at the Sands*. It's been called the "definitive portrait of Sinatra

Count Basie, Ray Bauduc, Bob Haggart, Harry Edison, Herschel Evans, Eddie Miller, Lester Young, Matty Matlock, June Richmond, and Bob Crosby, at the Howard Theater, Washington, DC, c. 1941.

COUNT BASIE

BORN August 21, 1904 in Red Bank, NJ

DIED April 26, 1984 in Hollywood, CA

INSTRUMENT Piano and Bandleader

FIRST RECORDED 1929

INFLUENCES James P. Johnson, Willie "The Lion" Smith, Fats Waller

RECOMMENDED LISTENING

April In Paris (Live) *(1955)*

Count Basie at Newport *(1957)*

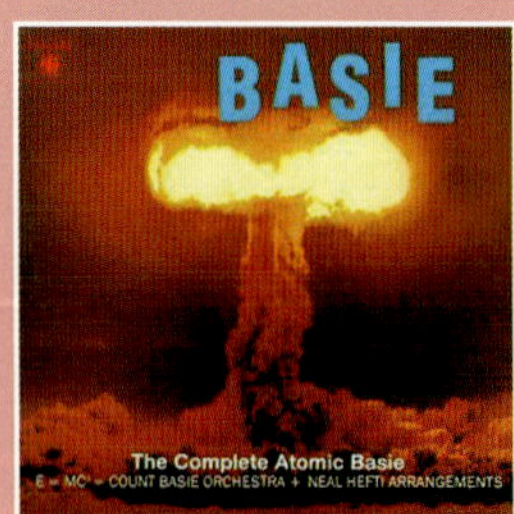

Atomic Mr Basie *(1957)*

Jazz icons - Count Basie Live In '62 DVD *(2006)*

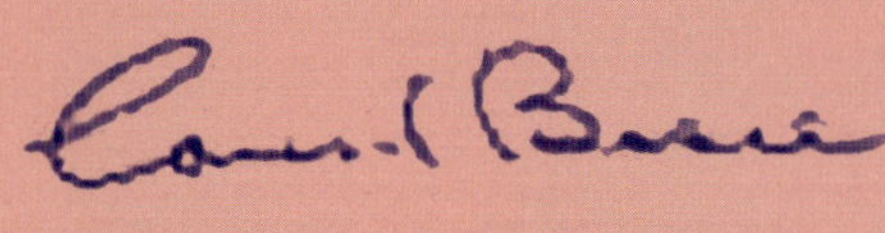

in the 60s." It's true, but likewise, it's a wonderful window on the great Basie band.

The Basie band kept working into the seventies, with the Count in his yachting cap that he had adopted in the sixties, but his age and changing fashion eventually caught up with him. Count Bill Basie died in Hollywood on April 26, 1984. His legacy is enormous: he may well have introduced more people over several generations to the sound of big bands than any other bandleader. Accessibility was key to his enduring appeal, but so was his ability to keep a great band together through his consideration for his fellow musicians and, in turn, the affection in which everyone held the Count. Today, there's no band that plays "April in Paris" without the musicians thinking of the man who just loved to swing.

Count Basie and Bob Crosby at the Howard Theater, Washington, DC, c. 1941.

WMCA

Tommy Dorsey & Frank Sinatra

"He was more than just a singer, he was a cultural expression of a whole nation's sense of style. He was our notion of class and elegance." *~ Jimmy Webb describing Frank Sinatra*

Take any event in world history and you can ask "what if?" Well, what if Tommy Dorsey had not signed Frank Sinatra to be his "boy singer" in 1940? Would Sinatra have become the "Chairman of the Board?" Or would he just have been another singer with the big bands, rather than greatest jazz singer of all time? Some of you will be thinking, of course he would – but perhaps you shouldn't be so certain.

Thomas Francis Dorsey Jr. was born in Shenandoah, Pennsylvania in 1905. His father, a part-time musician and coal miner, taught Tommy and older brother Jimmy to play the trumpet. Later, Tommy switched to the trombone, while Jimmy played clarinet and saxophone.

In the 1920s Tommy, like many of his contemporaries, played with Paul Whiteman's Orchestra, as well as the bands of Red Nichols, Joe Venuti, Ted Lewis and Vincent Lopez. In 1928 Tommy and Jimmy founded The Dorsey Brothers Orchestra. They had their first minor hit with "Coquette" the same year, and over the next six years they had a few more. It was in late 1934, when Glenn Miller was in their band, that they signed to Decca. During 1935 they released numerous records, having hits with "Lullaby of Broadway" and "Chasing Shadows."

Tommy, who had a quick temper, argued with Jimmy one night while they were on stage. He stormed off and soon took over the Joe Haymes Orchestra; from then on the brothers vied to be the best, a contest that Tommy won, but not by much. Tommy worked with brilliant and respected arrangers, including Sy Oliver, Paul Weston and Axel Stordahl. He was not slow to spot a good singer and good singers were eager to sing with his band; Jack Leonard handled vocals before Frank Sinatra got the job.

Frank Sinatra was born on December 12, 1915 in Hoboken, New Jersey and weighed in at an impressive

Tommy Dorsey, WMCA, New York, c. October 1947.

thirteen and a half pounds. He was in the breech position, which made for a very difficult birth. Frank's mother's problems with her son's birth meant she never had any more children.

After a childhood of comparative luxury, even through the Depression, Frank dreamed of becoming a singer. He won a talent competition with three other local lads, and they went by the name of the Hoboken Four. They even toured for a while until Frank fell out with the others. Home in New Jersey, he worked wherever he could, ending up at a roadhouse called the Rustic Cabin in early 1938, where he was both singer and MC. In 1939 he married Nancy Barbato, made a demo disc with the Frank Mane Orchestra, and the wife of bandleader Harry James heard him on the radio.

Harry's wife, the singer Louise Tobin, was packing and listening to the radio before leaving town to play some dates with her boss Benny Goodman. She heard Frank on the WNEW *Dance Parade* and told Harry that he ought to check out the singer. The next night Harry drove over the George Washington Bridge and headed for the Rustic Cabin, hopefully to meet the singer. "I asked the manager where I could find the singer."

After hearing Sinatra sing "Begin the Beguine," Harry offered him a job, and by the end of June 1939 Frank was singing with one of America's most popular bandleaders.

"We don't have a singer. We have an MC that sings a little bit." *~ The manager of the Rustic Cabin*

Sinatra recorded just ten songs with Harry James; the first two, "From The Bottom of My Heart" and "Melancholy Mood," were cut on July 13, 1939 in New York City, prior to an evening show at the Roseland Ballroom. None of these records were a hit during Frank's time with the band.

In late November 1939 Jack Leonard decided to leave Tommy Dorsey's band, despite (or because of?) having been voted the number one male band vocalist in the *Billboard* poll. Both the James and Dorsey bands were in Chicago at Christmas to play at a benefit for the Mayor. Tommy's manager slipped a note to Frank asking if he

Frank Sinatra at Liederkrantz Hall, New York, c. 1947.

"The Dorsey band could do more things better than any other." *~ Critic George T. Simon*

would meet Tommy in his suite the next afternoon.

When Frank and Tommy met at Tommy's hotel he offered Frank $125 a week; Frank accepted without hesitation. Tommy was the number two band in the land, after Benny Goodman. Frank straightaway went to Harry to tell him what had happened. Harry immediately agreed to release him and they ended their business relationship on a handshake.

Frank's first gig with Tommy was in Rockford, Illinois on January 26, 1940. Frank had to be on his metal as the boys in the band were in need of some impressing. According to Jo Stafford who sang with the Pied Pipers, Tommy's vocal group. "I never laid eyes on him until he actually walked on stage for the first time. He came on and sang 'Stardust' and it was quite an experience. Up until then, the great sound you were looking for was the always the Crosby sound."

Almost immediately, Frank was in the studio with Tommy to cut their first sides together. Dorsey and his fifteen-piece band backed Frank singing "The Sky Fell Down," which was arranged by Axel Stordahl, one of Tommy's regular arrangers. It was the first time that Frank worked with Axel and it was to be one of the longest running, and most fruitful relationships of Frank's career. In March "Polka Dots and Moonbeams" made number 18 in the *Billboard* chart for just one week at the end of April – it was Sinatra's first hit record.

While singing with the Dorsey band was not the happiest period of Frank's life, he quickly recognised the

"I first met Sinatra around 1939. I was playing trumpet with Charlie Barnett's band and we met up with Harry James' band. Frank was just another guy then… not outstanding at all." *~ Billy May, arranger and bandleader*

advantages; learning from his boss was probably the most valuable. Many have suggested that Frank copied Tommy's style of dressing, his manner of speaking and even his temper tantrums. But what was far more important was what Frank learned about vocal technique from Tommy's trombone playing. "The thing that influenced me most was the way Tommy played his trombone. He would play it all the way through, seemingly without breathing, for eight, ten, maybe sixteen bars. I used to sit behind him on the bandstand and watch, trying to see him sneak a breath. But I never saw the bellows move in his back. His jacket didn't even move. Finally I discovered that he had a 'sneak' pinhole in the corner of his mouth – not an actual pinhole, but a tiny place where he was breathing. He'd take a quick breath and play another four bars with that breath. Why couldn't a singer do that too?" Well Frank did and "The Voice" was born.

Tommy offered Frank some solid advice, advising him to listen to Bing Crosby. "All that matters to him is the words," said Tommy, "and that's the only thing that ought to matter to you." In October 1940 Tommy Dorsey's band headed west to Hollywood to film a Paramount comedy called *Las Vegas Nights*. At the same time the band were appearing on a new weekly radio show for NBC called *Fame and Fortune*. Later, they opened the Palladium Ballroom in Hollywood. They also appeared all over the country, including a month-long engagement at New York's Paramount Theater.

On August 27, 1941the Dorsey Band began another engagement at the Paramount in New York City. This three-week run was proof of Frank's burgeoning stardom – girls mobbed him, and his vocal spots became the highpoint of the show. It was around this time that Frank first considered a career away from Dorsey. Whereas big bands and their leaders had always been the stars, Frank sensed an opportunity to strike out on his own. He had a point, as of the fifteen Tommy Dorsey records that made the charts in 1941, only three didn't have Frank singing on them.

"Frank was not like a band vocalist at all. He came in self-assured, slugging on that first date, he stood his ground and displayed no humility, phoney or real." *~ Henry Myerson who supervised Frank's first solo session*

Early in January 1942 Frank made his first step towards freedom, although it was artistic rather than contractual. At RCA's Hollywood studio Sinatra recorded four songs with an orchestra conducted by Axel Stordahl. These records were to be released on Victor's budget label, Bluebird. Frank was obviously excited. According to Axel Stordahl "I'll never forget when we got the advance dubs on the first two sides. Frank had a room in the Hollywood Plaza. We sat in it all afternoon of a sunny day, playing the two sides over and over on a portable machine. He was so excited, you almost believed he'd never recorded before."

Dorsey and the band kept busy touring during the spring, and then in the early summer of 1942, Frank told Tommy of his intention to leave, but he was in no hurry and intended to stick around through the end of the year.

LAURA
VIOLINS
FRANK SINATRA

Tommy's immediate reaction was not recorded, but it is probable that he thought Frank might change his mind, or that things might change Frank's mind. He also had another card up his sleeve that might have made him relaxed about the whole idea. Later he said, "Let him go. Might be the best thing for me. Anyway I could get another crooner... Dick Haymes." During the 1940s many felt that Haymes was Frank's equal when it came to vocal ability, although most thought Frank could interpret and phrase a lyric better.

Frank officially announced his departure from Tommy Dorsey on August 28 at the Circle Theater in Indianapolis. On September 3 Frank bid farewell to the band on the air, handing over to his replacement, Dick Haymes. It was pure synchronicity, having done the same thing when he left the Harry James band.

During his two years with Dorsey, Frank recorded over ninety songs. It was an incredibly important time, which he would later acknowledge, although in the immediate aftermath, both men felt a good deal of resentment.

In 1942, Dorsey had hired Artie Shaw's string section to give his sound a revamp. In truth, the decline in the big band sound, albeit a slow one had began. In 1947 Jimmy and Tommy filmed the fictional movie *The Fabulous Dorseys*, before they formed the Tommy Dorsey Orchestra Featuring Jimmy Dorsey. Things looked up for a while and the band even had its own TV show in 1954. Elvis Presley made his TV debut on their *Stage Show* on January 28, 1956, but ironically, it was rock'n'roll that really finished off the big bands. But before Tommy himself could witness this shift in popular taste he died on November 26, 1956 in Greenwich, Connecticut choking to death in his sleep.

Within three months of leaving, Frank became the bobby-soxer's idol; within a year he was the original pop idol. He had taken Axel Stordahl with him to be his arranger, which was a shrewd move. In wartime America to love-lorn women, Frankie was their man; Frank was the Sultan of Swoon. There were riots in Times Square when he performed in New York, and when Frankie went to Hollywood to make a string of movies – most of which were at best average – even they couldn't dent his popularity.

He is thin-faced, tired looking, and carries that world-weary look which comes of being so long a totem of the tearful." ~ The Daily Express, 1951

Frank avoided the draft, but in the process stirred up an ill wind that would do him no good with American servicemen returning from overseas to their loved ones – many of whom adored Frankie. He was all over the radio, with shows beamed into the vast majority of American homes. He was also all over town, where he met Lana Turner and Marilyn Maxwell. On one of Frank's nights on the town he met a woman who would become his muse, and also very nearly his ruin; the gorgeous and sexy 22-year-old Ava Gardner.

With the war over and Frank still singing great songs and appearing in movies, including *Anchors Aweigh*, he was probably unaware of what was about to hit him. His involvement with the Mob is well documented, and often exaggerated beyond all credible belief. Yet there is no denying that he "consorted with criminals" as the FBI so eloquently put it. Eventually Ava and Frank began a tempestuous affair; even Hollywood was shocked. Meanwhile, the hits were becoming less frequent, and the

Axel Stordahl and Frank Sinatra at Liederkrantz Hall, New York, NY, October 22, 1947.

movies less well received. Frank trailed around the world after Ava, which of course did nothing for his career. He played shows in London in 1950, and Frank and Ava's antics prompted a Church of England minister to pass comment about "Painted trollops who worship at the shrine of Saint Ava Gardner."

In 1950 Frank's first TV series was a miserable flop, and the openness of his affair with Ava was by now just too open for most of America. The end of Frank's marriage to Nancy came in 1951, and he was finally free to marry Ava. But it was already a case of "be careful what you wish for." He even recorded a song called "Mama Will Bark" with an actress named Dagmar, popular more for her breasts than her acting talents, and a man impersonating a dog!

During the second half of 1952 things between Frank and his new wife got worse. Frank's lack of any decent work played havoc with their relationship. Ava was doing better than ever, having landed a part in the movie *Magambo*, which she filmed in Africa. While Frank was with her, mentally he was back in Hollywood because he was desperate to play the part of the loser Maggio in the movie, *From Here To Eternity*. He won the part, and while he was filming in Hollywood, Frank signed to Capitol Records and a month later made the classic "I've Got The World On A String." He hadn't quite got it yet, but within months the greatest singer of the twentieth century, or any other, had somehow done it… and the rest is history.

TOMMY DORSEY

BORN November 19, 1905 in Shenandoah, PA

DIED November 26, 1956 in Greenwich, CT

INSTRUMENT Trombone

FIRST RECORDED 1926

INFLUENCES Paul Whiteman

FRANK SINATRA

BORN October 26, 1913 in New York, NY

DIED May 14, 1998 in Los Angeles, CA

INSTRUMENT Singer

FIRST RECORDED 1939

INFLUENCES Billie Holiday, Mabel Mercer

RECOMMENDED LISTENING

The Song Is You
(The Complete Tommy Dorsey & Frank Sinatra Box Set) *(1994)*

Songs For Swinging Lovers *(1955)*

In The Wee Small Hours *(1954)*

Come Fly With Me *(1957)*

A personal appearance by Tommy Dorsey in a Washington DC record store. Also in the shot are Jo Stafford, Ziggy Ellman and Dick Haymes.

CAPITOL and COLUMBIA
RECORDS
TOMMY DORSEY
and His Orchestra
TOMMY DORSEY
and His Orchestra
EVENING STAR
HAND ME DOWN MY WALKIN' CANE
LONDONDERRY
DEEP RIVER
THE BAND PLAYED ON
DECCA
IRVING BERLIN
Here in Person
FRIDAY APRIL 4th at 3 15 P.M.

Gene Krupa

"Gene never turns and glares at you if you have a bad lip or hit a bum note. He just lets you play the way you know best, he never drives you." *~ Roy Eldridge*

Gene Krupa's place in music history, and drumming in particular, will be assured due to the fact that he was the first man to ever use a bass drum pedal in a recording studio back in 1927. He was also a very fine drummer, who was so famous from the mid-1930s until the 1950s, that Hollywood made a film about his life. He was a showman behind the kit, but a sober, serious and disciplined man away from the spotlight. In the early 1940s he said "Drum solos must have substance and continuity." It's advice that many drummers that followed him would have done well to have heeded.

Eugene Bertram Krupa's parents were Polish and their son, the youngest of nine children, was born in Chicago in January 1909. There was nothing in his family background to suggest that he would go on to become one of the big band era's greatest drummers. His first musical foray was with a sax but he switched to the drums when he was eleven. He was a teenager when he first began to play with bands around his home city. Later he made an impact in Chicago, when, in 1927, he auditioned with a talent agency and secured a job with Thelma Terry, becoming one of her Playboys.

After she and her husband had divorced, Thelma's mother had taken her daughter to Chicago from Bangor, Maine. Thelma was signed by MCA, the talent agency, and it was them that organized the auditions and changed her name from Combes to Terry. She and her band appeared at The Golden Pumpkin nightclub at 3800 West Madison in Chicago, and some people have suggested that that the newly named Playboys may have been the house band. Whatever the case, the teenage drummer was now backing the "Beautiful Blonde Siren of Syncopation" as she was billed.

The following year Krupa recorded with the Eddie Condon Quartet in New York, which may have happened while he was still with Thelma's Playboys, while they were on the road. Gene had already been in the studio a few months earlier in Chicago, recording with Thelma's band. They had cut five sides in March, but by the time that

Gene Krupa at the 400 Restaurant, New York, c. June 1946.

"The archetype of the layman's conception of a jazz drummer." ~ Benny Green

Thelma's band was back in the studio in New York in September, a couple of months after the Condon session, Krupa had left them.

In April 1929 Krupa worked for the first time with Red Nichols and his Five Pennies, again in New York. At that same session was Glenn Miller on trombone, and a twenty-year-old Benny Goodman on clarinet. After that Krupa didn't record again with Nichols, the most prolific recording trumpeter of the late 1920s and early 30s, until the January of the following year. At this session both Tommy and Jimmy Dorsey were in the band that was billed as Red Nichols and His "Strike Up the Band" Orchestra Nichols records sold in their hundreds of thousands, but he was also a hard-working band leader on a nightly basis. Krupa played with him at the Hollywood Restaurant on Broadway and 48th Street for much of late 1929, and by January 1930 they had became the pit band for the Gershwin show, *Strike Up The Band*. Also there were Goodman and Miller, which was fortunate for Krupa. Gene could not read music and so had to fake his parts during rehearsals. He learned them with Glenn Miller's help, who hummed them until Gene was perfect.

Over the coming years, Gene was heard with Bix Beiderbecke, Adrian Rollini and Joe Venuti on various recording sessions before once again working with Nichols in the pit band for Gershwin's musical, *Girl Crazy*. After a short spell with crooner Russ Columbo's band, he joined Benny Goodman's orchestra in early 1935.

Working with the Goodman Band was the making of Gene Krupa's reputation. He not only played with the main orchestra, which featured such great players as Ziggy Elman and Harry James on trumpet, but he also played with

Goodman's trio and quartet. The trio was Benny, Gene and black pianist Teddy Wilson, for the quartet Lionel Hampton was added on vibes. These were among the very first occasions that black and white musicians worked so prominently together. They did much to help change attitudes, although it was admittedly among the few rather than the many.

In July 1937 the Goodman band were recording out in Hollywood while they were working at the Palomar Ballroom; it proved to be an important event for everyone involved. They recorded a long tune stretching over both sides of o a twelve-inch 78, which meant that it clocked in at over eight minutes. It also featured drumming like no one had ever heard before. After the session the band also played their new recording live on the radio, which meant just about everyone who loved jazz loved "Sing, Sing, Sing."

In January 1938, the Goodman band became the first "jazz act" to play New York's Carnegie Hall. They featured "Sing, Sing, Sing" and Gene played an amazing extended drum solo, the first time such a thing had happened in jazz.

Gene Krupa, Washington, DC.

LEFT

However, there was a downside. All the attention paid to Gene meant that the spotlight was not on Benny and it caused tension between the two men. Two months later Krupa and Goodman parted company after a row at the Earle Theater in Philadelphia. A month later, Gene had his own big band, opening at the Steel Pier Ballroom in Atlantic City, where they were an instant hit.

Their first recording session happened almost simultaneously and featured Helen Ward who had been in the Goodman band, but they were more a vehicle for Gene's drumming than a sweet vocal band in the early days. Titles like "Drummin' Man," "Nagasaki," "Rhythm Jam" and "Wire Brush Stomp" give you an idea where they were coming from. Later, the band even featured a string section and grew to have almost forty members. For the Krupa band their equivalent of "Sing, Sing, Sing" was "Drum Boogie" which Gene reckoned was their most requested number over the years. They were also prolific in the studio, releasing a great number of records. Krupa gave singer Anita O'Day her first big break, and also got the brilliant trumpet player Roy Eldridge to join his band. It was in 1941, while they were in the band, that they were at their most popular.

The band did much to promote the Krupa name, but in addition he organized an annual drum contest with people participating from all across America. He also wrote a book on drum technique, which no aspiring drummer eager to enter and win the drum crown, would have failed to have read. He also appeared in several movies, including *Some Like It Hot*. Just when nothing could appear to go wrong Krupa was busted in Hollywood for possession of marijuana; he served almost three months in prison but was released when the man who had been the state witness withdrew his evidence. It all appears to have been something of a put-up job. When he was released, his friends were there for him and he played with both the Dorsey and the Goodman bands before reforming his own big band.

One little-known story of Krupa concerns his abhorrence of segregation and racial intolerance. In November 1941 his band were in York, Pennsylvania, when he got in an argument with a police officer. A restaurant had refused to serve the black members of his band and so Krupa got into a shouting match with them and the

" 'Sing, Sing, Sing', we started doing back at the Palomar on our second trip there in 1936. It was a big thing, and no one-nighter was complete without it." *~ Benny Goodman*

"The kids and the kittens shagged, trucked, jumped up and down and down and up, and often yelled and screamed at the series of sold killer-dillers." *~ A review of a Krupa gig in* Metronome *magazine .*

Gene Krupa drumming at the 400 Restaurant, New York, c. June1946.

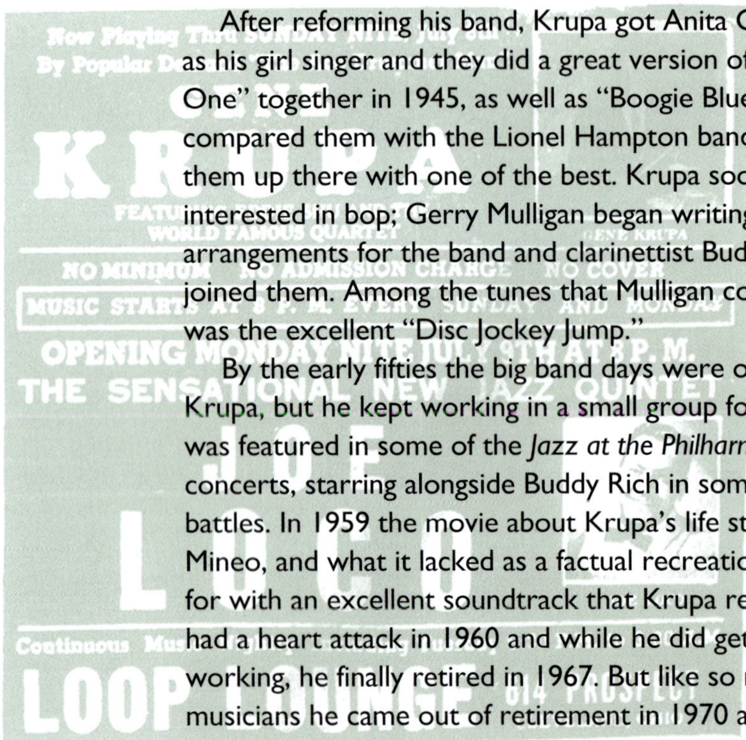

"I'm happy that I succeeded in doing two things. I made the drummer a high-priced guy and I was able to project enough so that I was able to draw more people to jazz."
~ Gene Krupa in later years.

policeman. He forfeited a $10 bond for failing to appear in court to answer a charge of disorderly conduct.

After reforming his band, Krupa got Anita O'Day back as his girl singer and they did a great version of "Opus One" together in 1945, as well as "Boogie Blues." Critics compared them with the Lionel Hampton band, putting them up there with one of the best. Krupa soon became interested in bop; Gerry Mulligan began writing arrangements for the band and clarinettist Buddy DeFranco joined them. Among the tunes that Mulligan contributed was the excellent "Disc Jockey Jump."

By the early fifties the big band days were over for Krupa, but he kept working in a small group format. He was featured in some of the *Jazz at the Philharmonic* concerts, starring alongside Buddy Rich in some great drum battles. In 1959 the movie about Krupa's life starred Sal Mineo, and what it lacked as a factual recreation it made up for with an excellent soundtrack that Krupa recorded. He had a heart attack in 1960 and while he did get back to working, he finally retired in 1967. But like so many great musicians he came out of retirement in 1970 and continued working until 1973. His last appearance was, fittingly, a reunion of the Benny Goodman Quartet. Two months later he died, having probably made more people take up drumming than most any of his contemporaries and possibly any single person since.

GENE KRUPA

BORN January 15, 1909 in Chicago, IL

DIED October 16, 1973 in Yonkers, NY

INSTRUMENT Drums

FIRST RECORDED 1928

INFLUENCES Tubby Hall, Zutty Singleton

RECOMMENDED LISTENING

Benny Goodman Live at Carnegie Hall 1938 *(1950)*

Drumming Man *(1947)*

Gene Krupa Volume 1 *(1954)*

Gene Krupa Plays Gerry Mulligan Arrangements *(1958)*

Stan Kenton

"Stanley Kenton is the leader and I am working with him. We do arranging and I think we have cooked up something new in style." *~ Ralph Yaw, one of Kenton's staff arrangers in 1941*

Stan Kenton, besides being a great bandleader and an inspired arranger, was also a great teacher through the university jazz clinics he established in 1959. It was this lasting legacy of "Stan the Man," as he was known to many jazz fans, that has reinforced Kenton as a jazz great. Having once threatened to quit the music business to become a psychiatrist, it is not surprising that above all else Kenton played thoughtful jazz. For many years he had, one of the most popular big bands in the world.

Stanley Newton Kenton was born in Wichita, Kansas in December1911, but by 1916 he and his family were living in Los Angeles. Apparently Stan's father was not around very much, allowing his over-bearing mother to dominate her son. It was she that gave young Stan his first piano lessons, but things only began to make musical sense for him when a cousin introduced him to jazz in the mid-1920s.

Even while he was still at school, he was playing semi-professionally at the same time as listening to records. One of the first recordings to catch the teenage Kenton's ear was Gershwin's *Rhapsody in Blue*. Released on record at the end of 1924 by Paul Whiteman's Concert Orchestra, with Gershwin himself playing the piano, it became an immediate hit. The piece, which was orchestrated by Ferde Grofé, had received its premiere in New York in February 1924 at a concert in the Aeolian Hall that was billed as *An Experiment in Modern Music*. It wasn't just the audacity and brilliance of Gershwin, Grofé and Whiteman that was to stay with Kenton for the rest of his life – the concert's title was to prove just as inspirational. Many of Kenton's later albums had titles that harked back to this seminal concert: *Artistry in Rhythm* and *Adventures in Jazz* to name just two

Before any of Kenton's ideas could take proper shape he had to earn his jazz stripes, and after leaving school he played just about anywhere, and with anyone, to learn his craft. His first regular band gigs were in the Depression years from 1933 to 1935 with two Californian groups led by Everett Hoagland and Russ Plummer; both were just a local draw. His first real opportunity came in May 1937 when Kenton, who had joined Gus Arnheim's Orchestra, headed east to New York to record with them for the Brunswick label. There were several more sessions over the course of the summer, in which Kenton sounded a lot like Earl Hines, which is exactly what Arnheim wanted him

"Within the Stan Kenton band nestles one of the greatest combinations of rhythm, harmony and melody that's ever been assembled." *~ Review of a Bilboa Beach gig in summer 1941 by George T. Simon.*

to do. Then they were back on the road for a few months before Stan quit the group to remain in Los Angeles to try to find work in the movie music business. Pretty soon he was back working with a band, this one led by his old friend Vido Musso. As well as playing piano with them, Kenton got the chance to arrange much of their material, which was important for his ambitions.

Musso's was never a hard-working band, as they did not have the profile of either regular radio work or recordings, and so Kenton began working at a Hollywood movie theater as pianist and conductor of the house orchestra, work that has been described as "lucrative but stagnant." This was probably the worst period of his career, matched only be the very early years of playing dives around Los Angeles, but at that time he was too young to know any better. Stan's only way out was to do his own thing, and so in late 1940 he set about forming his own band. They had their debut at the Rendezvous Ballroom in Balboa Beach on May 26, 1941, playing there regularly throughout the summer. The kids who hung out at the beach loved the Kenton band and became avid and vociferous supporters. Here was a new kind of swing – not swing à la Goodman, or the swing of Artie Shaw, but symphony swing.

Later, Kenton explained how his shows were highly organized, programmed down to the last detail to get the maximum dramatic reaction from the audiences. "Everything was written to swing to a driving beat, spirit and enthusiasm had to predominate at all times. I figured that 11.30pm to midnight was our high period. Our climax was so complete that if you had touched any kid in the audience, I think he would have thrown off sparks."

Soon Decca signed the band, putting them in the studio to record four sides in September, among them "Adios," "The Mango" and "Taboo." All are proto-Kenton sound because the producer made them tone down their performance to appeal to what he thought the record-buying public wanted. Around the same time, the Stan Kenton Sax Quartet recorded the ambitious *Suite for Saxophones*, which even incorporates a tip of the hat to *Rhapsody in Blue* on "A Reed Rapture." It also included "Opus in Pastels" as one movement within the suite, which become a staple of the Kenton band over the coming years. At a later Decca session they did manage to

Above: The Rendezvous Ballroom in Balboa Beach, 1938.

Right: Stan Kenton, Pete Rugolo, and Harry Forbes, Capitol studio, c. Jan. 1947.

"He was so personal, always one of the fellows and yet nobody ever lost any respect for him." *~ Shelly Manne, Kenton's drummer for several years.*

swing and sound more like the live Kenton band, but after the attack on Pearl Harbor in December 1941, America's attention was focused, for a while at least, on more important issues. The Kenton Band struggled for a while, even managing to get pulled from an eight-week engagement at New York's Roseland Ballroom after only three weeks.

For the next couple of years the Kenton band battled to make headway and began to attract some negative press from some who complained their sound was over-blown and pompous and not jazz at all. Eddie Condon

"Stan Kenton was incredible. When he spoke people listened. He had presence." *~ Art Pepper*

Johnny Mercer

even claimed that for every Kenton recording date it sounded like he'd signed three hundred men "who all turned up and just played on time." The disheartened Kenton almost quit the business, but the as often happens, he got his big break just when he needed it. Bob Hope's radio show was just about the biggest thing in broadcasting in 1943, and Kenton's band got the job of house band after Skinnay Ennis had to leave to join the army. It was a break that worked financially, but it attracted yet more criticism.

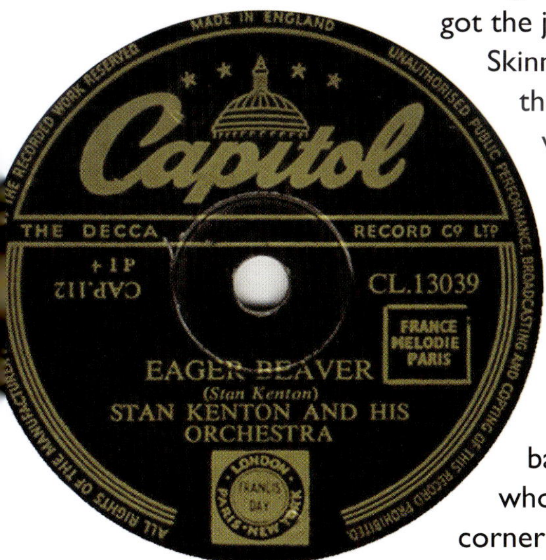

Whether it was hearing him on the radio or just being attracted to his sound on records, or live in one of Los Angeles' ballrooms, Glenn Wallichs, who owned Music City on the corner of Sunset and Vine, decided to sign Kenton to the new label he had started with songwriter Johnny Mercer, the lyricist on standards like "That Old Black Magic" and "Blues in the Night." Ironically their first release on Capitol Records had been "The General Jumped At Dawn" by Paul Whiteman's Orchestra. The Kenton band cut Ellington's "Do Nothing 'Til You Hear From Me" and Cootie Williams "Concerto for Cootie"; the Ellington song made the *Billboard* Top Ten in February 1944. The band on these records was very different from the 1941 line-up and many of the changes were necessitated by wartime call-ups. Among the latest recruits was an eighteen-year-old sax player named Art Pepper who said that Kenton, "reminded me a lot of my dad."

For the next six years Kenton had a run of hits on the Billboard charts, as well as being a big live draw. "Eager Beaver," "Artistry in Rhythm," "Tampico" (a million-seller with its June Christy vocal) all did well and with the hits came better bookings. Anita O'Day had originally joined

"Stan was trying to do a different kind of music. . .They were concert pieces with a jazz sound." *~ Pete Rugolo*

the band as singer, and she was later replaced with June Christy. The brilliant Kai Winding came in on trombone, Buddy Childers who had joined as a sixteen-year-old in 1943 blossomed into a star, and Shelley Manne came in to play drums. Kenton found a young composer/arranger named Pete Rugolo, prompting Stan to exclaim, "My God, he writes just like I do." It was Rugulo that helped reshape the band's sound for the last five years of the 1940s and on into the fifties; he worked on many of the "Artistry" albums that became their standard output.

During late 1946 and early 1947, Kenton's career had stumbled because of his marital problems, and he paid off his band in order to take a complete break. When he re-formed in September it was with many from his old Artistry in Rhythm Orchestra, but this time he named it the Progressive Jazz Band and went off in something of a new direction. Titles like "Chorale for Brass, Piano and Bongo" and "Elegy for Alto" give you an idea of what Stan was thinking of with his new sound. Yet again, there were those among the critics who claimed it was not jazz, some even claimed it was not even music. But the band was

Stan Kenton and his Orchestra with Laurindo Almeida, 1947.

proving as popular as ever with fans; they won the *Downbeat* poll and also wowed audiences at the Hotel Commodore as 1947 ended. During the month they also recorded "The Peanut Vendor" which became one of their most popular records.

A first trip to Europe in 1953 was a huge success, although Britain missed out on that occasion because of the stringent Musicians' Union laws that stopped many American artists from playing for their British fans. Kenton did return in 1956 for a five-week UK tour; it was a sell-out.

In 1959 Kenton established his jazz clinics at Indiana and Michigan State universities, and from then on much of his efforts focused on the teaching of music at university. He did not turn his back on the commercial world and won Grammies for his *Adventures in Jazz* and *West Side Story* in the early Sixties. While the debate about Kenton's contribution to jazz has never been settled, there's no denying that he nurtured talent in his bands. Other arrangers who worked with Stan include Neal Hefti, Johnny Richards and Bill Russo. Among those who started out with the Kenton band are Zoot Simms, Maynard Ferguson, Stan Getz, and Lee Konitz, besides those already mentioned.

The man whose arrangements are among the most widely used of any arranger, both by stage bands and university bands, died in August 1979. His legacy will continue as long as big bands continue to play music and the debate about just how jazz is Stan Kenton will probably go on for just as long.

STAN KENTON

BORN December 15, 1911 in Wichita, KS

DIED August 15, 1979 in Los Angeles, CA

INSTRUMENT Piano and Bandleader

FIRST RECORDED 1928

INFLUENCES Earl Hines, George Gershwin

RECOMMENDED LISTENING

The Stan Kenton Story *(2000)*

In Concert *(1956)*

West Side Story *(1961)*

Adventures In Jazz *(1961)*

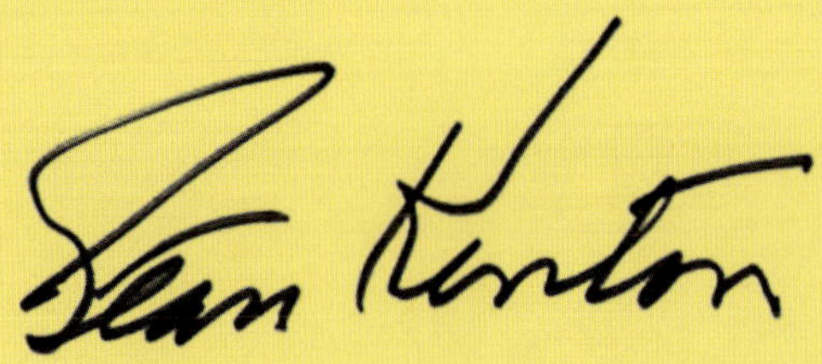

Charlie Barnet

"The band business was a romping, stomping thing and everybody was swinging." *~ Charlie Barnet*

There are some who wish to endlessly debate whether or not big bands play jazz, or whether or not it's something else that we should call "dance band" or "swing band" music. The fact is you can dance to jazz, it swings – sometimes – and some of the bands that played jazz were big. Charlie Barnet's band most certainly exuded spontaneity and could ad-lib with the best jazzers around. His band was colorful, carefree, and some have even called it a little crazy.

Charles Daly Barnet very definitely didn't come from the wrong side of the tracks. His was not an upbringing steeped in poverty, one where music was a means of escape. In 1915 his parents divorced when he was two, so his mother and grandparents brought up Charlie. His mother's family were very wealthy and he was sent to a smart boarding school and was expected to go on to Yale. Charlie had other ideas, however – he wanted to blow his saxophone in a band – big or small.

Charlie's family had only themselves to blame. In 1925, when he was twelve years old, they gave him a sax, one known as a Melody-C, a kind of a cross between a tenor and an alto. Charlie learned to play by listening to records while playing along with his favourite – Coleman Hawkins, the saxophonist with the Fletcher Henderson band.

Charlie Barnet started out playing for other band leaders and even played on a transatlantic liner, crossing the ocean a number of times when he was still a teenager. He was soon fronting his own band, taking them into a New York studio a little over two weeks before his twentieth birthday to record four sides. The material was well arranged and well played, but it lacked that vital spark to set the Barnet band apart from the rest of the dance band pack. They worked at the Paramount Hotel Grill in Manhattan and for the next few years Charlie and his band were kept busy playing live, recording a few more records, but all the while failing to get very much attention. As well as playing sax, Charlie also sang pretty well, as he did on the band's recording "Emaline" in 1934.

The shape of things to come came when Barnet, still a month shy of his twenty-first birthday, recorded two sides with vibraphone player Red Norvo and his Swing Septet

"When I heard Hawkins play, I just naturally switched to tenor." *~ Charlie Barnet*

"A happy-go-lucky millionaire, living it up and making money talk."
~ Billie Holiday

followed by another two sides a week later. Barnet had worked with Norvo at the Paramount Grill, and among the tunes the Septet recorded were "The Night is Blue" and "I Surrender Dear"; on both tunes Charlie plays very well. With him on those sessions were the then unknown Artie Shaw on clarinet and Teddy Wilson on piano. Benny Carter also played on some of Charlie's band sessions. In early 1935 Barnet had met the saxophonist and trumpet-playing bandleader in 1934 and it was through him that the Barnet band came to play a week at Harlem's Apollo Theater – this was the Harlem venue at which very few white artists got the chance to appear

While the Norvo sessions were a pointer, everything changed once Charlie fell under the spell of Duke Ellington's music, and they went from being a relatively "sweet" sounding band to a really swinging affair. Barnet was clever, copying Ellington's style and arrangements so well that one critic called them, "The blackest white band of all."

With his film star looks, it was perhaps none too surprising that Charlie headed west to appear in several movies. They were small parts and the lure of Hollywood soon wore off and he was back in New York in 1936 at the Glen Island Casino. He recorded under their name for a little while, but was soon performing under his real name.

Barnet's family background provided the money to make his dreams come true, but it would be wrong to think he was just a playboy who indulged his passion. While the Barnet band did seem to have far more fun than many of their contemporaries, it's an image that belies the fact that they always played great music, were disciplined in their work, and Charlie created an atmosphere in which creativity was allowed to flourish.

Barnet's band was not just black in spirit because Charlie had, over the years, many black musicians go through his ranks. It's a factor that many believe kept Charlie off of the radio for quite a while, because some commercial sponsors were less than happy with his mixed band. Equally, hotels that operated a segregated policy failed to book the Barnet band because they felt their clientele would be offended by the sight of a black and white band. To his eternal credit, Charlie stuck to his principals. Having rebelled against his family by becoming a professional musician, this was, of course, not uncharacteristic.

In late 1936 the band had their first modest hit, "Sing, Baby, Sing," from the movie of the same name; Charlie provided the vocals, and while it may not be jazz as we know it, it helped to got their name out there. It would be another three years until the Charlie Barnet band became a

"The most forceful, driving reed instrument in the world."
~ Metronome *critic on Charlie Barnet's tenor playing.*

Charlie Barnet at a WOR broadcast from the Aquarium, New York, c. August 1946.

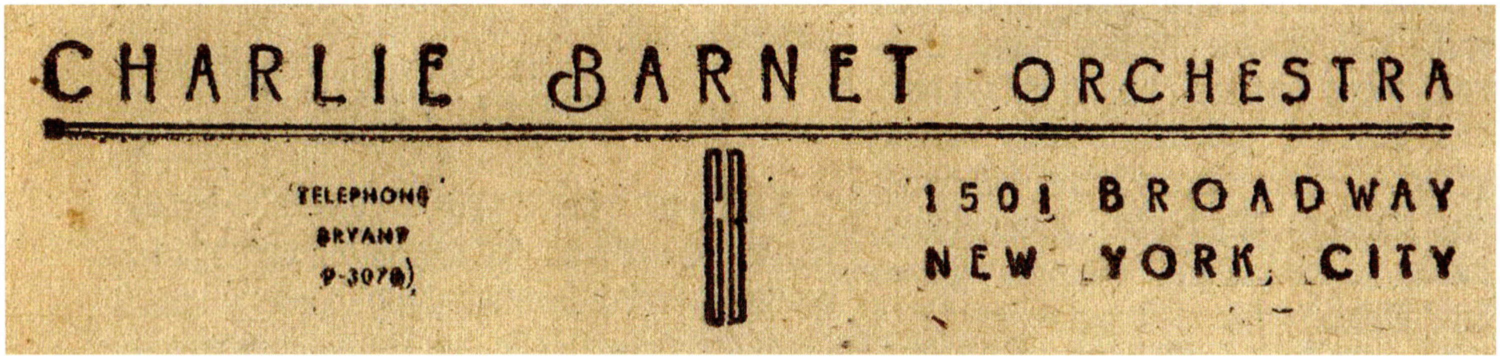

household name throughout America. Having taken over Count Basie's residency at The Famous Door on 52nd Street, the band had a minor hit with "Knockin' at the Famous Door." It's as good an indication of how good they were as a band to have followed the Count. By the summer of 1939 the band were hot and were drawing good reviews from the respected *Metronome* magazine.

While the band were getting rave reviews, not everything in their working life went to plan. They were playing the Palomar in Los Angeles when it caught fire and burned down. No one was hurt, but all the band's on-stage suits and their instruments were lost, as was their precious sheet music with all their arrangements. Both Duke Ellington and Benny Carter sent them copies of their own band's arrangements so they could fulfil their engagement prior to getting new dots drawn up.

Proof of Charlie's great "ears" was when he hired trumpet player and arranger Billy May. Billy, a fun-loving guy fitted in right away, but he also provided the arrangement for "Cherokee," which became a big hit in the autumn of 1939, as well as the band's theme song; allegedly Billy May wrote the arrangement while travelling on the band bus. It was one of over fifty recordings they made that year. The following year they worked even harder, both in the studio and on the road, having another big hit with May's arrangement, "Pompton Turnpike," a song that featured in *The Sopranos* on television in 2004.

Towards the end of 1940 Barnet again ignored what was considered sensible, if he wanted to work everywhere, by hiring Lena Horne, a black singer. Yet again his musical taste over rode any consideration of discrimination. While Lena didn't stay long with the band, it was something that she never forgot.

By the end of 1941 Barnet had parted company with the Bluebird label where he had most of his recording success,

"It was Charlie who took a chance to give me my first real break." *~ Lena Horne*

Charlie Barnet at a WOR broadcast from the Aquarium, New York, c. August 1946.

of Vanity Fair

to sign with Decca. Changes in personnel included Dizzy Gillespie playing with the band for a while in 1942 but unfortunately never recording with them. By this time the music press was applauding Barnet for his mixed-race band, although reporters and commentators for jazz magazines in particular were always at the forefront of the race debate in America. As one said, "(Barnet) is doing a lot to break down racial prejudice."

The difficulties of keeping a band together through the strictures of war-time America affected Barnet just like everyone else. While he didn't need to work for a living, others did, so it was no surprise that as the war was nearing its end the band just about broke up. However, this was not before there was one last big hit record – the brilliant and exciting "Skyliner," a song that Barnet co-wrote.

By 1946 he was back on the road, but it was a hard sell. It was around this time that these photographs were taken, but they had, according to Cliff Leeman who had recently rejoined the band, passed their prime. "We were at a terrible loss for a while – musically. We'd lost our original sound." They were more a bop band than a swing band, although they had some fine musicians including Clark Terry. Over the coming decade, Charlie, having moved to Palm Springs and the Californian sunshine in search of something new, did keep playing, but he was more often found playing golf and fishing. There was one thing that Charlie never gave up on and that was women. He always had a beautiful girl on his arm and married six, ten or eleven times, depending on who you believe.

Come the 1960s and Charlie did front a big band on occasions and even recorded some albums for the Creative label, but by this time he really was swimming against the tide. Charlie's own words probably sum up his views on jazz and probably life. "I like to hear the beat. To me jazz should be exciting. Remember there's a difference between 'exciting' and 'startling'."

Charlie Barnet with yet another beautiful girl on his arm.

CHARLIE BARNET

BORN October 26, 1913 in New York, NY

DIED September 4, 1991

INSTRUMENT Soprano, Alto and Tenor Saxophone

FIRST RECORDED 1933

INFLUENCES Coleman Hawkins, Duke Ellington, Johnny Hodges

RECOMMENDED LISTENING

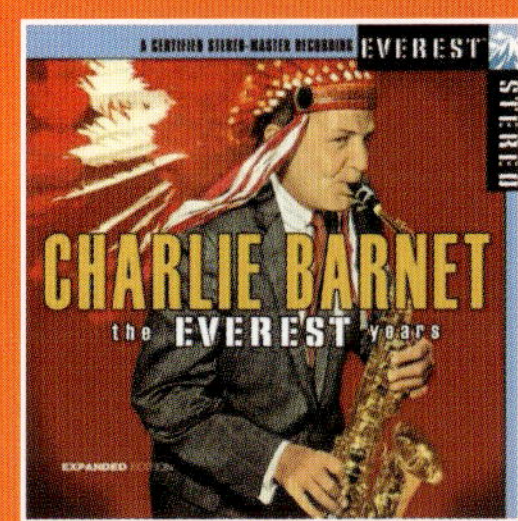

The Everest Years *(2005)*

Cherokee *(1999)*

Rockin' In Rhythm *(1954)*

BILLIE HOLIDAY

"With a few exceptions, every major pop singer in the US during her generation has been touched in some way by her genius." ~ *Frank Sinatra*

Today, legendary artists seem to be ten a penny. Back when Billie Holiday was first accorded the accolade, it really meant something. "Lady Day" was a brilliant singer, a great lyrical interpreter, she took chances, lived life hard, she could swing, she could swoon, she moaned low, was elegant and she was a soul singer before anyone had coined the phrase. Added to which, she was one of the greatest jazz vocalists of all time. She really is a legend.

Eleanora, the daughter of Sadie Harris was born on April 7, 1915; that much we know. After that the facts about Billie Holiday's childhood get a little murky, made no clearer by *Lady Sings the Blues*, Billie's autobiography, which, if anything, only helped to confuse things further with its somewhat stylized recounting of the story. Billie's birth certificate named her father as a local waiter named DeViese, whereas she always insisted that he was in fact Clarence Holiday who had been Sadie's childhood sweetheart from Baltimore. Clarence later played guitar in Fletcher Henderson's orchestra.

What we also know is that Billie's childhood was difficult, including her being abused, by a neighbor aged eleven, after she was left at home by Sadie while she went to work. A spell in a Catholic children's home stabilized things for a while, before she went back to her mother. This is probably when Billie began doing some cleaning, as well as running errands for a brothel madam. By 1928 Sadie moved to Harlem where Billie joined her; before long they were both working in a whorehouse. Billie was charged with vagrancy a month after her fourteenth birthday and sent to a workhouse for one hundred days.

On her release Billie took up with a saxophonist named Kenneth Hollon and the two of them played and sang in dives and other low life joints around Harlem; Billie tried to emulate Bessie Smith, whose records she loved. By 1930, or soon after, she was working at a club in Brooklyn, before moving to another club named Pods; later still she worked in a popular nightspot in Harlem called Jerry's, frequented by jazz enthusiasts. In 1933 things began to look up for Billie, when John Hammond, a music critic, record producer and lover of jazz, heard her.

Almost immediately Hammond took Billie into the studio to record a couple of sides with Benny Goodman.

Billie Holiday at the Downbeat, New York, c. February 1947.

"I was big for my age, had big breasts, big bones." *~ Billie Holiday*

The first was at a session on October 18, 1933, but "Your Mother's Son-in-Law" gives no real hint of her promise. The other songs that Goodman recorded that day were with blues singer Ethel Waters. Two months later, a few days before Christmas 1933, Billie did "Riffin' the Scotch" with Goodman, which is better.

It would be a year or more before Billie would record again. This time Hammond had coerced Brunswick into funding a session. The records were released as Teddy Wilson and his Orchestra. The musicians once again included Benny Goodman, along with saxophonist Ben Webster, drummer Cozy Cole, Roy Eldridge on trumpet and Wilson himself on piano. Billie, who had not long turned twenty, recorded "Miss Brown To You," "What a Little Moonlight Can Do," "I Wished Upon the Moon" and "A Sunbonnet Blue." Every song is a gem and should be in every jazz enthusiast's library. The light and airy playing of the band perfectly complements Billie's elegant, and by now fast-maturing, vocals. At the end of July they went back into the studio in New York, this time without Goodman, but largely the same band, and recorded another batch of wonderful tunes, the standout being, "It's Too Hot For Words."

"Billie, why don't you just sing some blues?" *~ John Hammond at the July 10 session.*

Over the next twelve months Billie recorded about a dozen more sides with Teddy Wilson, before going into the studio under her own name, with her own orchestra. The first session was on July 10, 1936 and she did four songs including the beautiful "Summertime" and "Billie's Blues." The orchestra comprised Bunny Berigan on trumpet, Artie Shaw on clarinet, Joe Bushkin on piano, Dick McDonough on guitar, Pete Peterson on bass and Cozy Cole on drums; they created a fabulous sound.

Another session followed in September, followed by two in January of 1937, one with Billie's own orchestra and another with the Wilson orchestra. At the session for Wilson on January 25 were Buck Clayton on trumpet, Goodman, Wilson, guitarist Freddie Green, Walter Page on bass, Jo Jones on drums and the incomparable Lester Young on tenor sax ≠ it was a superb band. The four songs included the lovely "This Year's Kisses" and "I Must Have That Man." Recording with Teddy Wilson continued until 1942 and the tunes are rightly considered among the most important in jazz music.

In 1937 Billie sang with Count Basie's orchestra, and the following year she appeared with Artie Shaw, becoming one of the first black singers to perform with a white orchestra. It was not an easy engagement for either Shaw or Holiday. When the Shaw orchestra played in Kentucky, she was abused by a member of the audience, and it ended in a small-scale riot. By the end of the year a disenchanted Billie had quit Shaw's band after the Hotel Lincoln in New York demanded that she use the kitchen entrance rather than the front door

"Simply The Best." ~ *Artie Shaw*

like the rest of the band.

Whatever Billie's personal difficulties, there was no doubting her influence on other singers as others adopted her airy, light approach to singing. It wasn't just the women singers that Billie influenced. Frank Sinatra worked on his vocal technique by visiting New York nightclubs, like the Uptown House. Frank told the *Melody Maker* that he, "First heard her (Billie) standing under a spotlight in a 52nd Street jazz spot. I was dazzled by her soft, breathtaking beauty." Frank later recorded many songs that Billie had previously made her own.

After her spell with Artie Shaw, she began appearing at Café Society in Greenwich Village, which helped her cross over to an even larger white audience, as the club was not segregated, allowing everyone through their doors. Billie's performances at Café Society amazed all that heard her, they were especially enamored with the torch songs including "I Cover The Waterfront," which Sinatra would later record. However, there was one song that became synonymous with Billie's spell at the club. One night a New York public school teacher named Lewis Allen spoke with Barney Josephson, the owner of Café Society, about a song he'd written and asked if she would perhaps sing it. She readily agreed and so began the fascinating tale of "Strange Fruit."

Allen's song was about the lynching of a black man somewhere in the Deep South; it pulled no punches. The anti-lynching protest poem set to music is incredibly powerful and Columbia, Billie's own label, refused to release it. It did get made, released by the much smaller Commodore label, and when it came out opinion was sharply divided on the song, but there is no doubting its impact, especially when she sang it live. Audiences would be stunned into silence, while men as well as women were seen to weep.

Billie's career was progressing, with her releasing songs that included the classic, "God Bless the Child," but her personal life had long been less than she probably hoped for, although given her background, the odds were always stacked against her. She had several relationships, including one with Freddie Green the guitarist and then in the summer of 1941 she ended up marrying Jimmy Monroe who could at best be described as a hustler, and at worst something much more sinister. In 1942 he was caught trying to smuggle drugs into California and, despite Billie hiring the best lawyers, he got a one-year sentence. Monroe was smuggling marijuana, which Billie had been

" 'Strange Fruit' provided the National Association for the Advancement of Colored People a prime piece of musical propaganda." ~ Time *magazine, June 12, 1939*

"Billie took her homage like a queen. Her voice, a petulant, sex-edged moan, was stronger than ever." *~ Newspaper report of the Carnegie Hall concert*

smoking for years. He also brought opium into her life and by 1944 she was using heroin. It wasn't Monroe who introduced her to heroin, but a trumpet player with whom she had an affair when Monroe was sent to prison for a second time.

One of Billie's biggest successes was when she signed to Decca Records in 1944 and released "Lover Man." It was a song that resonated with many servicemen overseas, and particularly with their wives and lovers back home. By 1946 Billie was being seen as more than just a singer and she was offered a part in *New Orleans*, a film that also featured Louis Armstrong. It was about the birth of jazz, a typical Hollywood affair in which she performed "Farewell to Storyville" with Satchmo. At the end of the year an "album" of four 78s was released of the ballet *Fancy Free*. Written by Leonard Bernstein, who also conducted the orchestra it also featured Billie Holiday singing "Big Stuff." *Time* magazine described it as "The jaunty, jazzy ballet score with inappropriate lyrics sung-by blue-voiced Billie Holiday." This proved to be the biggest earning year of Billie's career to date, as she earned $50,000, well over a $1 million in today's terms.

Billie's drug problems finally caught up with her in May 1947, when she was arrested in Philadelphia and charged with possession of heroin; she received a one-year sentence at a Federal Reformatory in Virginia. When Billie was released she had kicked her habit and looked better than she had done in a years. A few years earlier one magazine described her in less than flattering terms: "Billie Holiday is a roly-poly young colored woman with a hump in her voice. She does not care enough about her figure to watch her diet." Almost immediately after she left prison a concert was arranged at Carnegie Hall in March 1948 in celebration; it was a sell-out. She sang over thirty songs, despite not having sung for nearly a year, including "Billie's Blues," "All of Me," "Fine and Mellow," and naturally "Strange Fruit."

Jimmy Monroe, the man who the federal prosecutor at Billie's trial described as the "worst type of parasite you can imagine," lost no time in getting Billie back into her

"(Fans) treating her in a manner so deferential that she reacted accordingly. Her morale was never better." *~ Leonard Feather*

Billie Holiday at the Downbeat, New York, c. February 1947.

bad habits. She was even arrested again on a similar charge to her conviction, but this time she was acquitted. Before long, a new man entered her life. John Levy was a club owner and was just as bad as Monroe. He controlled Billie's life and she was very definitely dependent on having a strong man around her. Levy was also a useless businessman, leaving Billie stranded with no money while on tour on at least one occasion. Despite everything, *Metronome* magazine named Billie the best female singer in its annual poll in 1949.

In the early fifties, with Levy in her life, things were something of a roller coaster, but in 1954 Billie did tour Europe and seemed happier than she had been in years, perhaps because she also had a new lover named Louis McKay, who at least kept drugs out of her way. The music critic and jazz-lover Leonard Feather got to know Billie and helped arrange the European tour. "I assembled a show called *Jazz Club USA* with her as the star, and the Red Norvo Trio, the Buddy De Franco Quartet, and the all female trio of the pianist Beryl Booker. We opened in Stockholm in January 1954. In place of the ghetto theaters and sleazy dressing rooms that had marked too much of her life at home, Holiday soon found herself besieged by autograph hunters, by fans bringing her bouquets onstage."

By 1956 Billie published *Lady Sings The Blues*, which received some good reviews but it was a fictionalized account of her life written with a journalist named William Duffy. Nevertheless, one review got it just right when they said, "Billie sings a sad, sad song." She also recorded for the Verve label, but these recordings were a pale shadow of her earlier work. They sound like a singer who hears what's right in her head, but doesn't have the voice to deliver what she's hearing. Billie at her best in these later years can be heard on the Columbia album, *Lady in Satin*.

In 1957 Billie married Louis McKay and, while things initially went well, fights between the two became more common, especially after Billie found out he had lost much of her money in risky property speculation. He was also upset by the fact that Billie was back on the drugs. They split up soon afterwards and Billie moved into an apartment in New York with just her dog for company. Her drug habit, which was by now fortified by excessive drink turned her into a pale shadow of her self.

When Lester Young, probably her one true friend throughout her life, and the man who had given her the name "Lady Day, died in March 1959 it was the last and hardest blow for Billie. Two months later she was in

Billie Holiday at Carnegie Hall, New York, NY, March 16, 1948.

POWDER

"She could express more emotion in one chorus than most actresses can in three acts." ~ Jeanne Moreau

hospital having collapsed from drug use. She had been refused entry to one hospital because she took drugs and even in this second one, where they were more tolerant, it was toleration that did not extend to the actual taking of drugs while being treated. A nurse found drugs at her beside in early June and called the police. Despite being in hospital she was arrested. Just over a month later Billie Holiday died, still in hospital, still under arrest.

Billie Holiday was a complex person who could exasperate her friends beyond all belief, but at other times she was the sweetest natured woman alive. Before the drugs, the booze and the lifestyle of an addict ravaged her voice and her body, she could sing with such intensity and with such soul that she transcended people's belief about just how moving a singers voice could be. What's for sure is we'll never see anyone like her again. Although it seems like every generation throws up one, two or three Billie Holidayesque singers, none of them have the gift to do what really matters most – to sing like you really mean it.

Billie Holiday and Mister, her pet Boxer, New York, NY, c. June 1946.

BILLIE HOLIDAY

BORN April 7, 1915 in Philadelphia, PA

DIED July 17, 1959 in New York, NY

INSTRUMENT Singer

FIRST RECORDED 1933

INFLUENCES Bessie Smith, Ethel Waters, Louis Armstrong

RECOMMENDED LISTENING

***Lady Sings The Blues** (1956)*

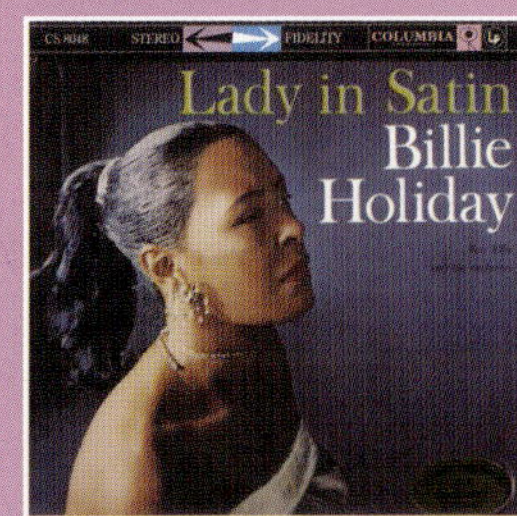

***Lady In Satin** (1958)*

***The Commodore Master Tapes** (2000)*

***20th Century Masters - The Best of Billie Holiday** (2002)*

Ella Fitzgerald

"She was the best singer on the planet." ~ *Mel Torme*

If Ella Fitzgerald had possessed the looks to go with her sublime voice, then unquestionably she would have been the most talked about, admired, revered and loved female singer of the twentieth century. As it was, she was simply the best women singer of jazz or any other kind of music . . . and one of the most loved.

Ella Jane Fitzgerald was born in Newport Mews, Virginia on April 25, 1917; her parents were not married and separated soon after her birth. When Ella was a few years old, she and her mother, along with her mother's new man, moved north to New York City. In 1932 Ella's mother died and soon afterwards her aunt took her into her own home in Harlem to spare her from the harsh treatment of her step-father. The fifteen-year-old Ella hated her Harlem school and skipped it as soon as she could to work as a collector for the illegal Mafia-run lottery. Tracked down by the authorities, she was sent to a Catholic school, but soon ran away, returning to Harlem where she lived rough on the streets.

Her life on the streets brought her into contact with others in the same situation, and her new friends encouraged her to enter one of the regular talent competitions at the newly opened Apollo Theater. Having gone there with the intention of dancing, she was intimidated by the standard of the competition and decided she would instead sing. It was one of those momentous decisions that really did change the course of her life. Passing the audition, the seventeen-year-old found herself singing with the Benny Carter Orchestra on November 21, 1934. She was no overnight sensation, but it convinced the teenager that this was what she would like to do for a living .

Eventually she got a job as the singer with Chick Webb and his Orchestra, but only after his male singer did a lot of cajoling on Ella's behalf. Her job was not just to sing – she also had to dance during the many instrumental numbers. In June 1935 Ella went into the recording studio with the Webb band for the first time, where she recorded two songs, "I'll Chase the Blues Away" and "Love and Kisses." Both are standard mid-thirties band arrangements, with Ella sounding young and enthusiastic but far from great.

Chick Webb had contracted tuberculosis of the spine while he was a child, leaving him both extremely short, as

"The best way to start any musical evening is with this girl. It don't get better than this." ~ *Frank Sinatra*

Ella Fitzgerald, New York, NY, c. November 1946.

"I never knew how good our songs were until I heard Ella Fitzgerald sing them." ~ Ira Gershwin

well as suffering from a badly deformed spine. He was born in Maryland, but moved to Harlem in his teens and by twenty-one he was leading his own band. Given his physical difficulties, it's surprising that he managed to become a drummer and a very good one at that. He drew admiration from many other bandleaders – Buddy Rich spoke of Webb as an inspiration.

In 1936 Ella had her first hit with "Sing Me A Swing Song (And Let Me Dance)." It's a much better song than her first two efforts and Ella sounds a lot more confident having had a whole year as a singer with a big band. As well as singing with Chick Webb, she performed on records with the Mills Brothers in 1937. Her big break came singing with Webb's orchestra in June 1938, when "A-Tisket A-Tasket" spent ten weeks at No.1 on the *Billboard* chart. It was probably a sign of the times when Ella and Chick had a hit a few months later with "Wacky Dust," an unabashed opus to cocaine. The following year Webb died aged just 34 ,and for a while Ella continued to front his orchestra, as well as recording solo.

However, it was a struggle as the band members were somewhat demanding and Ella, barely in her twenties, found them difficult to rebut. The band did have a manager, but the issues of what to play and in which direction to take the band, fell on Ella's shoulders. Enter Benjamin Kornegay, who, from doing the odd job for Ella, ended up marrying her the day after Christmas in 1941. The arrangement did not last long as it became clear that Kornegay was little more than a cheap hustler and an ex-convict with a drug problem – too much wacky dust probably – and the marriage was annulled.

Early 1942 saw the final demise of the old Chick Webb band that had become known on record and live as, Ella Fitzgerald and Her Famous Orchestra. Professionally, Ella formed a successful short-term partnership with the Ink Spots and they had two No.1 records in 1944, including the million-selling "Into Each Life Some Rain Must Fall." But her career was far from flourishing. She did successfully record with both Louis Armstrong and Louis Jordan in 1946, these were minor records, not big hits. Her 1947 recording of "(I Love You) For Sentimental Reasons" with the Delta Rhythm Boys became a hit;"My Happiness" with the Song Spinners was her biggest seller for many years, while "Baby It's Cold Outside" with Louis Jordan in 1949, from the Esther William's film *Neptune's*

Ella Fitzgerald, New York, November 1946.

Daughter, rounded out the decade. Of course what's obvious about all the "hits" is the fact that Ella always sang with others – no one could quite work out what to do with the "plump chanteuse," as one critic dubbed her, as a solo singer.

One aspect of Ella's commercial failure was the fact that she abandoned commercial recording for much of the last part of the decade, choosing, instead, to work with Dizzy Gillespie and becoming enamored with be-bop. She recorded a stunning version of "Oh, Lady Be Good" in 1947 with Bob Haggart. Compare it to her later songbook recording from over a decade later, and you hear two very different singers. Ella's scat singing almost defies belief. The same goes for "How High The Moon"; in Ella's hands the song becomes hers and hers alone. Charlie Parker was another she really admired, and while Dizzy and Ella's tour did good business at the box office, their work together was never going to sell a million records. Nevertheless, they sold out a show at New York City's Carnegie Hall, appeared at the Downbeat in Manhattan and had a very affectionate, though not romantic, relationship. Ella married Ray Brown, Dizzy's bassist, in December 1947 – it was life reflecting art as he played be-bop.

In 1949 Ella made her first appearance at the legendary Jazz at the Philharmonic series of concerts. It marked something of a watershed in her career, as Ella from this point on seemed to rise above the fray, to elevate herself to a higher musical plane. As the 1950s rolled around Ella's appearances on the Billboard charts became infrequent, but this was by no means a reflection of the quality of her recordings. Songs like "I've Got a Crush On You" were stunning, and pointed the direction in which Ella was going. The public liked them too, which meant that by 1954 she had sold over 20 million records which put her up with the most popular singers, black or white; most importantly she was way out in front of all the other black singers.

Her career was further helped by Norman Granz, the man who founded *Jazz at the Philharmonic*, when he signed Ella to his Verve label; he set about taking her career to yet another level. The little girl who had slept rough in Harlem must have pinched herself when she found herself singing in the best concert halls around the world. Ella's rise to what we now call superstardom was masterminded by Granz, who devised the songbook series of albums in which Ella sang her way through the Great American Songbook, composer by composer, starting

"These albums were among the first pop records to devote such serious attention to individual songwriters, and they were instrumental in establishing the pop album as a vehicle for serious musical exploration." ~ The New York Times

Ella Fitzgerald watched by Dizzy Gillespie, Ray Brown, Milt Jackson, and Timmie Rosenkrantz at the Downbeat, New York, c. September 1947.

with Cole Porter. The album quickly sold 100,000 copies in 1956.

It is her work with the Verve label and the eight songbook albums that have become the basis for her continuing popularity. The fact is that these albums represent the pinnacle of Ella's art and an achievement that is matched by a mere handful of singers or any other artist for that matter. The mood she creates with material that is as good as you can get, has meant that for many of these songs sung by Ella are now the definitive versions. Take "Manhattan" from the Rodgers and Hart songbook; Ella's phrasing when she goes into the chorus is transcendent. If you've never heard it, take a listen, your life will never be the same again

These Songbooks had arrangements by the likes of Nelson Riddle, Buddy Bregman, Billy May, Duke Ellington and Paul Weston. Both Ellington and Billy Strayhorn, the Duke's long time collaborator, appeared on the songbook of the bandleader's songs. The Songbooks have been called a major contribution to American culture. Given jazz's position as the art form that America has given to the world, that places them just about as high as you can get in the canon.

"I realized then that there was more to music than bop. Norman felt that I should do other things, so he produced the Cole Porter Songbook for me. It was a turning point in my life." ~ Ella Fitzgerald

Ella's last US chart success of any note was "Mack The Knife," which managed to make No. 27 in 1960; the significance of this to the singer was probably of little consequence. What any chart placing did for Ella was to introduce her to some new listeners, possibly younger ones, to whom she was just a name on their parents' ageing LP. Ella is one of those singers that younger listeners discover as they get a little older, sometimes it's when they fall in or out of love. Ella, like all the

Impressario and Verve Records boss Norman Granz, who founded the Jazz at the Philharmonic concerts.

great singers, talks to people through her songs. She makes a song's lyrics mean things, whereas in the hands of less talented singers they are just words arranged over a catchy melody.

If Ella had a secret, it was her diversity. She had started out a swing singer, moved to be-bop, she sang perfect scat, was an extraordinary jazz vocalist and had no fear of modern material in the 1960s and 1970s. From the blues to bossa nova, and calypsos to carols, she imbued them all with her unique voice, sounding forever young. She was blessed with a three-octave range, and diction and enunciation that was like Frank Sinatra's – perfect.

Ella's personal life was never the match for the songs that she sang. Her marriage to Ray Brown lasted barely five years and that was the last time she married. By 1986 she needed open-heart surgery and in 1992 she had both legs amputated below the knees as a result of complications arising from diabetes. In 1991 the First Lady of Song, having famously once said, "the only thing better than singing is more singing," gave her final concert at New York's Carnegie Hall. Lady Ella died five year later, leaving the world a better place thanks to her ability to sing and swing better than it seemed possible for anyone to do.

ELLA FITZGERALD

BORN April 25, 1917 in Newport News, VA

DIED June 15, 1996 in Beverly Hills, CA

INSTRUMENT Singer

FIRST RECORDED 1935

INFLUENCES Connie Boswell

RECOMMENDED LISTENING

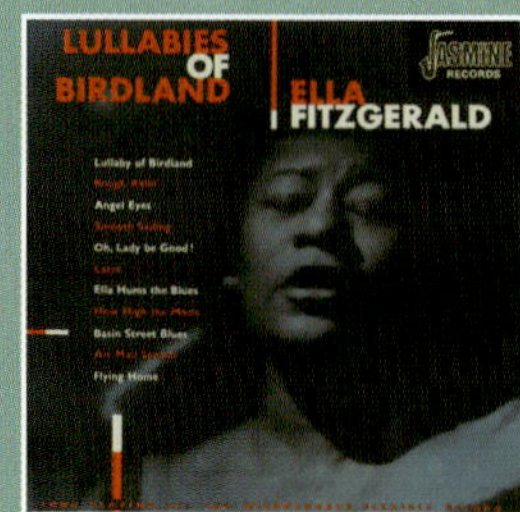

Lullabies of Birdland *(1954)*

Ella Sings the Rodgers & Hart Songbook *(1956)*

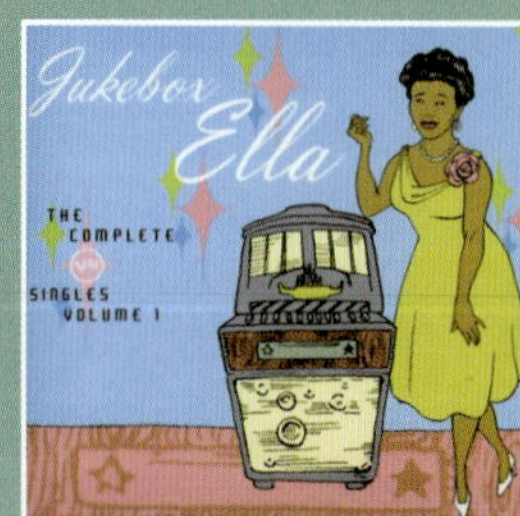

The Complete Verve Singles *(2004)*

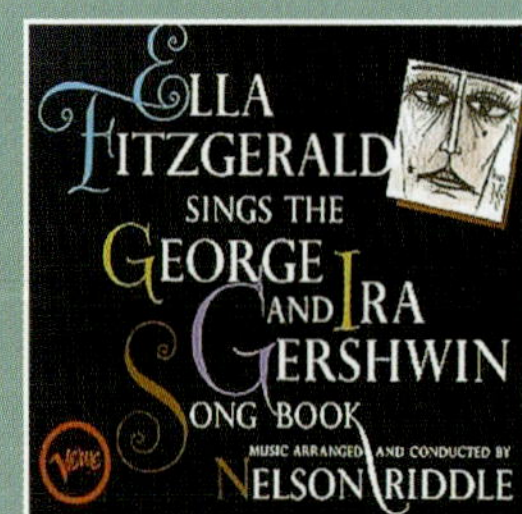

Ella Sings the George & Ira Gershwin Songbook *(1959)*

Thelonious Monk

"Though Monk's career has been painful and often thankless, it has also been a tortoise-and-hare race with flashier, more ingratiating men – many of whom got lost in narcotic fogs, died early in squalor and disgrace or abandoned their promise, to fall silent on their horns. Monk goes on." *~ Barry Farrell,* Time *magazine, 1964*

He might just be the most misunderstood pianist in the history of jazz, he might also be the most brilliant. He created a jazz world entirely of his own making. It was original, strange, illogical, and for some people it was not jazz at all; for others, it was ground-breaking, it was single-minded – it was Thelonious Monk.

Thelonious Monk was born October 10, 1917 in Rocky Mount, North Carolina, but at age four moved with his family to New York City. Monk's father was musical, and it is likely that this is where Monk got his early interest in the subject, but he was also an athlete in school; he began by studying piano when he was ten years old. Like many other pianists of his generation and background, he played organ in church, but at the other end of the musical and spiritual spectrum, he became a pianist for a traveling faith healer; later he played piano at house rent parties. These affairs were very common in the twenties and thirties when people got together to "pass the hat" to help pay the rent and to give a share to the musician(s). Without these gatherings, that originated in Harlem and spread through the black communities, especially in the South, the development of both jazz and the blues could have been very different.

His first professional work was playing Minton's Playhouse in Harlem, having been encouraged by pianist Bud Powell, who although he was Monk's junior, had began his professional career much earlier. There was a nod to Bud in 1947 when Monk began recording under his own name and he cut "In Walked Bud." Monk may well have recorded with the house band, but no-one is quite certain. What everyone is sure about is the fact that this famous Harlem club played host to musicians that included Don Byas, Charlie Parker, Dizzy Gillespie, Mary Lou Williams, Max Roach and Roy Eldridge, and they, along with others, were at the forefront of the emerging be-bop style of jazz.

"Anybody can play a composition and use far-out chords and make it sound wrong. It's making it sound right that's not easy." ~ Thelonious Monk

What is certain is that Monk entered the recording studio with the Coleman Hawkins Quartet in 1944, cutting a few titles. Some of the saxophonist's fans complained about their hero's eccentric pianist; what was also clear is that the veteran jazzman sensed the pianist's greatness. Monk had moved to the Spotlight Cub on 52nd Street and it was while he was here that he wrote "Round Midnight" with Cootie Williams that the trumpeter recorded. It was in 1947 that Monk made his first recordings with a sextet, which he did for the Blue Note label. Among the music was the self-titled, *Thelonious*, and this was the opening salvos of a five-year relationship with the label that produced some stunning records.

"People would be calling his changes wrong to his face… but he always went his own way and wouldn't change for anything." ~ One of Monk's early sidemen.

Because Monk played jazz piano differently from any other pianist, certainly before and probably since, jazz fans were unsure what they were listening to. It produced some furious exchanges in the music press on both sides of the Atlantic –certainly in those sections of the press that tried to understand what was going on with jazz. Monk just ploughed his own furrow; his philosophy was simple, "play your own way. Don't play what the public wants—you play what you want and let the public pick up what you are doing, even if it does take them fifteen, twenty years." As the fifties began, Monk also played with Charlie Parker on a number of recordings. Among the standout tracks is the beautiful "My Melancholy Baby." In 1951 an arrest for narcotics possession meant that he lost his cabaret card, a requirement for performing in New York clubs, which made life difficult for a while and caused a loss in earnings.

Throughout this period Monk experimented with new concepts of harmony and rhythm, and by 1953 he had signed to Prestige Records, which some critics have decided was his least fruitful period. Nevertheless, there were some amazing moments among his recordings. None more so than a session on Christmas Eve 1954 when he recorded *Bags' Groove* with the Miles Davis All Stars. This record became one of the cornerstones of the post-bop movement. In the same year he also appeared at the Olympia in Paris, which introduced him to a new group of jazz disciples across the Atlantic.

Having been anointed as "the high priest of bebop," Monk was never content to confine himself to one jazz genre, as his recording with Miles proves. In his own recordings and in his compositions he was soon entering uncharted territory; some in the jazz fraternity were not pleased that either he or they were making the journey. 1955's "Gallop's Gallop" was just too way out for some, as was his work with Art Blakey for others. Then, just to get things back on track, and to at least return some of

Thelonious Monk at Minton's Playhouse, New York, NY, c. September 1947.

"Thelonious Monk plays it strange and beautiful because he feels strange and beautiful." *~ Hampton Hawes*

the doubters to the fold, he recorded three LPs of sheer brilliance. There was the aptly named *Brilliant Corners*, *Thelonious Himself* and an album with tenor saxophonist John Coltrane. Some even claimed that these albums made him the most controversial figure in jazz, others, quite rightly, see them as pivotal moments in jazz piano or any other kind of jazz for that matter. It was during 1957 that Monk played a long-term gig at the Five Spot Café in New York City with Coltrane.

What was different about Monk was that he utilized the entire keyboard of the piano, every black note, every white note. He even used silence to create a kind of music that had never been heard before. Some have argued that it was his ability to have both the simple and the complex together in the same piece, others feel that it is his humour, while others are certain that Monk's music is all about his chord construction. The truth is that it's all of those things and more. It's music that makes the audience think and it also made the musicians that Monk played with think very hard when they worked together.

"When Thelonious Monk played the Apollo in the late 1950s he wore a pink sequinned neck tie – his one concession to the demands of show business. " *~ Ted Fox in Showtime at the Apollo*

According to John Coltrane, "I learned new levels of alertness with Monk because if you didn't keep aware all the time of what was going on, you'd suddenly feel as if you stepped into a hole with no bottom to it."

By the last years of the fifties Monk was enjoying one of the best periods in his career. He was touring extensively in America and Europe, and he ended the decade with a concert at the Town Hall in New York with an orchestra playing arrangements of his compositions done by Hall Overton. The early sixties saw frequent touring, commercial and critical acclaim, and a new recording contract with the more mainstream Columbia Records. His albums during this period included *Monk's Dream* and *Straight, No Chaser*; he even had his photo on the cover of *Time* magazine – one of only three jazz musicians to ever have achieved such status.

Thelonious Monk, Howard McGhee, Roy Eldridge, and Teddy Hill at Minton's Playhouse, New York, c. September 1947.

MINTON'S PLAYH

650

"All musicians are subconsciously mathematicians."
~ *Thelonious Monk*

By 1970–71 he was touring worldwide, including a spell with the Giants of Jazz that included Dizzy Gillespie and Art Blakey. He recorded an album in London, which some critics hailed as yet another departure for the Monk – jazz explorer. However, before anything could become of this new venture Monk disappeared off the music scene and seemingly off the planet. He did make a couple of appearances at the Newport Jazz Festival in 1975 and 1976, but other than that there was silence. During this time he lived in New Jersey with his friend and patron, Baroness Pannonica de Koenigswarter.

Many conflicting stories have been put forward as to why Monk was absent. They range from drug theories, both his own use of them and the inadvertent taking of LSD; others talk of brain damage, most people agreed there were mental health issues. The fact is that he didn't play in public, and those who appear to be in the know think he didn't play in private either, after his 1976 Newport appearance, until he died in February 1982 from a stroke.

Whatever the theories, the circumstances or the truth, the one fact is that the world lost a great and gifted musician – a true jazz visionary. But he has left behind a body of work that offers a jazz landscape more diverse and more challenging than most of his contemporaries. Sure, there are other jazz artists who played it obscure, but none of them played it half as well or half as interestingly as Thelonious Monk. The world is catching up with Monk. In 1993 he won a posthumous Grammy and in 2002 a Pulitzer Prize special citation. He's no doubt up there, doing it straight… no chaser.

Thelonious Monk, Minton's Playhouse, New York, c. September 1947.

THELONIOUS MONK

BORN October 10, 1917 in Rocky Mount, NC

DIED February 17, 1982 in New Jersey, NJ

INSTRUMENT Piano

FIRST RECORDED 1944

INFLUENCES James P. Johnson, Duke Ellington

RECOMMENDED LISTENING

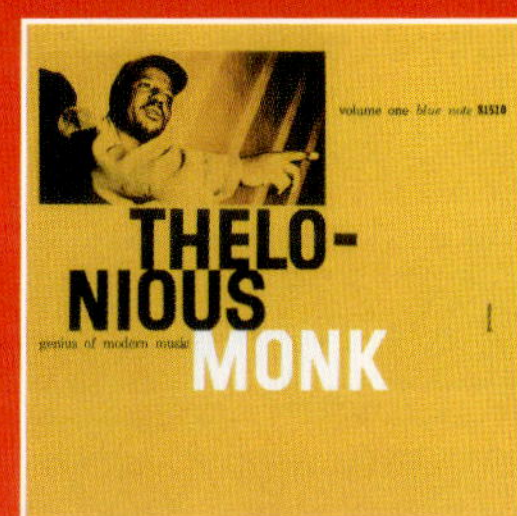

The Genius of Modern Music Volume 1 *Blue Note 1947*

The Genius of Modern Music Volume 2 *Blue Note 1947*

Brilliant Corners
Riverside 1956

Thelonious Monk with John Coltrane *Riverside 1957*
Grammy Hall of Fame

Monk's Music
Riverside 1957

Nat King Cole

"He wasn't corrupted by the mainstream. He used jazz to enrich and renew it, and left behind a lasting legacy. Very like a king." ~ Time *magazine*

He was dubbed the "Sepia Sinatra" in the 1940s because he was the only challenger to Frank Sinatra's role as America's premier singer. With his jazz leanings, his blues undertones, and a voice as smooth as silk he appealed to just about everyone, black or white.

Nathanial Adams Coles' family moved from Montgomery, Alabama, where he was born in 1919, to Chicago before he was five years old. His father was a preacher, and as a child he sang in church, encouraged by his mother who was an amateur pianist. His ability to "pitch-perfect" and natural talent to quickly pick out a tune on the piano made it seem inevitable that Nat was bound for a life in music. His father was none too keen on the idea of a life spent playing the sort of jazz and blues that his son liked to listen to on the radio

His older brother Eddie, who played bass, encouraged him, and soon the two were leading a band that played on Chicago's south side. Things seemed to come to abrupt halt for sixteen-year-old Nat when Eddie left to join an orchestra in New York. However, that didn't last long and Eddie was soon back in Chicago, relaunching the brothers' band as as Eddie Cole and His Solid Swingers.

Nat made his recording debut in July 1936 for Decca with brother Eddie's band and the influence of Earl Hines' playing style, particularly on "Honey Hush," can be heard in the piano breaks. Nat also had his own band and he would frequently play Hines' arrangements. Soon after Nat recorded for the first time, he left Chicago and ended up in Los Angeles, at the beginning and the end of Route 66, which would become one of Cole's biggest hits in1946. He had fallen for a dancer named Nadine, who had persuaded the producers of a revival of Eubie Blake's revue, *Shuffle Along* to let Nat play the piano. The show was touring and on the way the two of them got married. Although the show was far from successful, by the time they arrived in California they decided to stay.

Playing up and down the California coast, Cole began to gain a solid reputation and Nat in particular was drawing admiring comments from the jazz fraternity and particularly other piano players who marvelled at his talent. He gained the moniker "King" from a club owner, which certainly stuck. Eventually, Nat was offered a residency at the Swanee Inn on North La Brea Avenue, just south of Hollywood Boulevard. The place was small so a three-piece was the only option – the King Cole Trio

Nat King Cole, New York, c. June 1947.

"All the musicians dug him. We went there just to listen to him because nobody was like him. That cat could play! He was unique." *~ An unknown musician who saw Nat King Cole in the Los Angeles clubs.*

was born. Nat enlisted bassist Wesley Prince and guitarist Oscar Moore to play with him, an inspired choice as both men were well known in the Hollywood studios – and the three of them got on really well.

The first time they recorded in 1939 they did so as King Cole's Swingsters, and over the next three years they laid down some great jazz as the King Cole Trio, with songs such as "Hit That Jive Jack" and "I Like To Riff," that are firmly rooted in the genre. Then in July 1942 Cole recorded with saxophonist, Lester Young and bass player Red Callender. Amongst the sublime sides were "I Can't Get Started," "Tea For Two," and "Body and Soul." The impeccable performances and especially Nat Cole's piano-playing show off his jazz credentials and instantly negate any critic who sees the man as just a "nice crooner."

In November 1942 the King Cole Trio recorded "That Ain't Right" which went to No.1 on the R&B charts. The following year "All For You" repeated the success, as well as crossing over onto the *Billboard* chart. A switch to the newly formed Capitol Records brought national recognition when, in early 1944, "Straighten Up And Fly Right" became a big hit; it was apparently the theme of one of his father's sermons. Later in 1944 Cole appeared at the very first *Jazz at the Philharmonic*, along with Illinois Jacquet, Jack McVea and other jazz stars.

Following his switch to Capitol, Nat King Cole was rarely off the *Billboard* best sellers' list. While he worked with big studio orchestras from 1946 onwards, his earlier work owed more to the juke joints than to the ballrooms and concert halls. After playing at the Paramount in New York with the Stan Kenton Orchestra in 1946, Cole got a radio series, becoming one of the very few black performers to get commercial sponsorship during a period when "white was still right" as far as advertisers were concerned.

Nat's drift away from his roots continued and there was a change in his personal circumstances when he divorced Nadine and married Maria Ellington. His new wife's background was solidly professional Boston, a good deal more upper class than showbiz, despite the fact that Maria sang with Duke Ellington's Orchestra – although he was no relation. Such was Cole's success on Capitol that it was the revenue from the sales of his recordings that helped the label to become so important.

In 1948 Cole recorded "Nature Boy" with a string orchestra, and it was a smash hit. The song's composer, eden ahbez (he liked his name spelled in lower case) lived, so legend has it, underneath the first L of the 'Hollywood' sign on Mount Lee in the Hollywood Hills. Born Alexander Aberle in Brooklyn, New York in 1908, Ahbez

Nat King Cole in his dressing-room at the Paramount Theater, New York, c. November 1946.

"Madison Avenue is afraid of the dark." *~ Nat Cole on why advertisers didn't support his TV show.*

had written his song about a "strange enchanted boy" "who wandered very far" only to learn that, "the greatest gift was just to love and be loved in return." One day Ahbez hustled Nat Cole's manager, giving him a manuscript copy of the song. Cole immediately recognized the old Jewish melody of the song, but liked the words and decided to record it. It's arguably the song that changed Nat Cole from a jazz singer to a popular singer.

Nevertheless, his influence had spread to many jazz piano players, including Errol Garner, Bill Evans, Charles Brown and Ray Charles. For the next two decades Cole was one of the biggest stars on the R&B charts, and no slouch on the mainstream *Billboard* charts, as his records increasingly crossed over to the white audience. Interestingly, one of his best-known songs, "Unforgettable" (recorded in 1951), was not one of his biggest single releases.

In the fifties and sixties Cole recorded with both Nelson Riddle and Gordon Jenkins, like his Capitol label mate Frank Sinatra; for a while he was even bigger than Sinatra because in the early fifties, before Frank signed to the Los Angeles label, Cole could do no wrong. He also

Wesley Prince, Oscar Moore, and Nat King Cole at the Zanzibar, New York, c. July 1946.

appeared in several movies during the Fifties, including *St. Louis Blues* in which he played W.C. Handy the self-proclaimed "Father of the Blues." He also had his own television series but the issue of his color may have prevented him from becoming more successful on the small screen.

For such a mild-mannered man and a singer of some of the most romantic ballads to come out of the 1950s, it's perhaps strange now to think that Cole should find himself at the center of some very unpleasant controversy in 1956. Cole was on tour with the British bandleader, Ted Heath and his orchestra in Alabama, when he was attacked by some white men for daring to appear on the same bill as a white band. Rather than trade insults with some bigoted sections of the community, Cole decided to do things in a different way. He supported the Civil Rights movement financially, culminating in 1963 when he announced that he was giving $50,000 (equivalent to $400,000 today) to organizations fighting for civil rights in the South. He pledged the money from his concerts in Los Angeles sponsored by the National Association for the Advancement of Colored People. His gesture encouraged other black performers to do likewise.

A heavy smoker, Cole was diagnosed with lung cancer in 1964. He died the following year, aged 45. In March 2000, with Ray Charles as his presenter, Nat King Cole was inducted into the Rock and Roll Hall of Fame. The man who once said, "Critics don't buy records. They get 'em free," was a twentieth-century great who died far too young. He left us with one of the most interesting recording legacies, ranging from pure jazz to sublimely romantic ballads.

Wesley Prince, Nat King Cole, and Oscar Moore, New York, c. July 1946.

NAT KING COLE

BORN March 17, 1919 in Montgomery, AL

DIED February 15, 1965 in Santa Monica, CA

INSTRUMENT Piano and Vocals

FIRST RECORDED 1936

INFLUENCES Earl Hines

RECOMMENDED LISTENING

Penthouse Serenade *(1952)*

Complete After Midnight Sessions *(1957)*

Nat King Cole Sings / George Shearing Plays *(1961)*

Big Band Cole *(1999)*

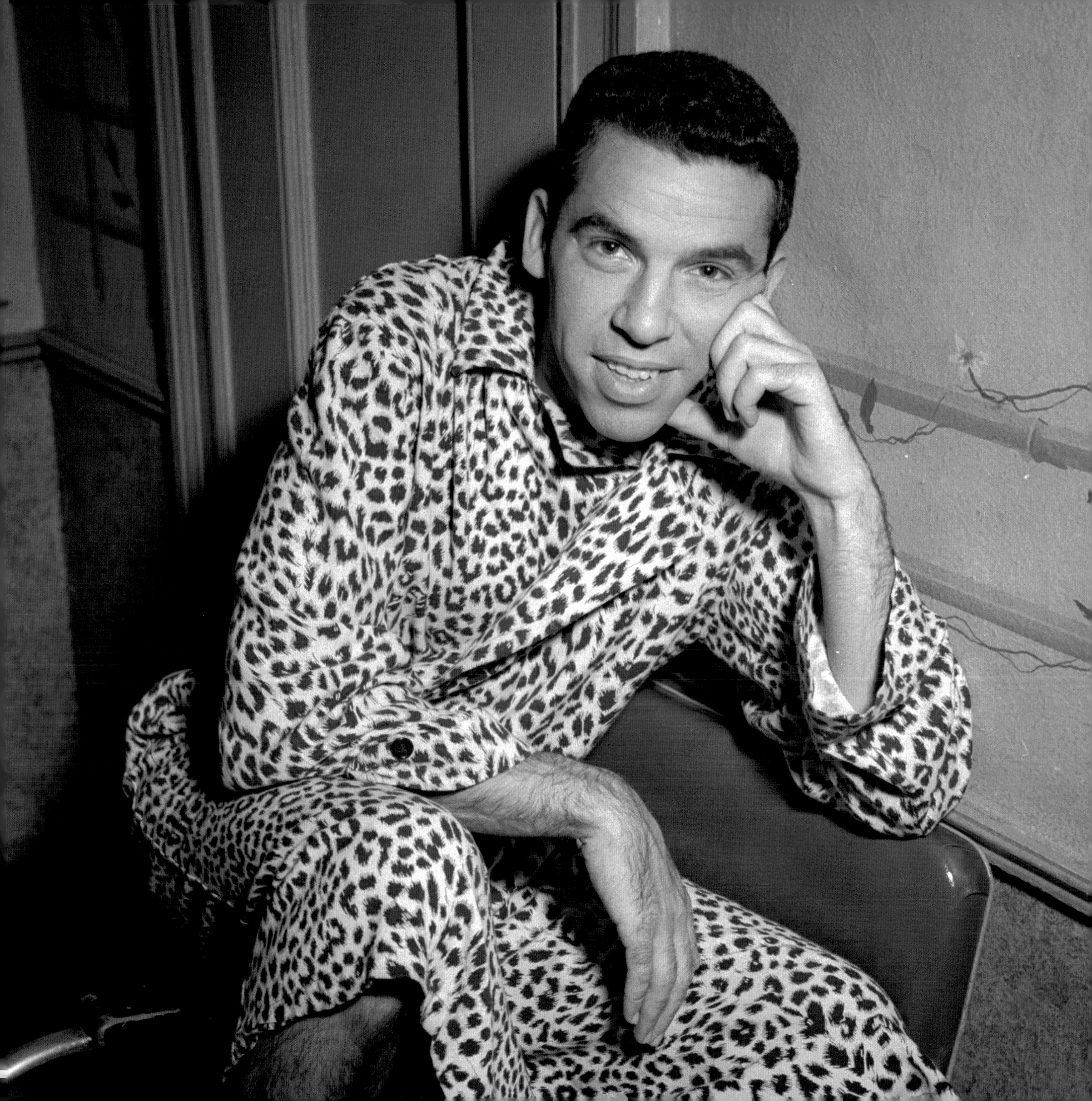

BUDDY RICH

"He was an amusing ebullient kid, and sometimes he would get so excited when he was playing that he would yell and rush the beat." ~ Artie Shaw

Deciding who is the greatest anything in jazz is always guaranteed to create lively debate among fans and musicians alike, but there's no doubt that Buddy Rich is one of the greatest drummers of all time. His career spanned seven decades, beginning before he was two years old and lasting until his death in 1987. Rich was gifted, could play with remarkable dexterity, despite never having had a drum lesson, and he always denied he ever practised.

Bernard "Buddy" Rich was, some might say, born to be on stage. His parents had a vaudeville act and he appeared with them before he was two years old, billed as "Traps the Drum Wonder." By the time he was four he had appeared on a Broadway stage, both drumming and tap dancing; at six years old he'd been on tour and been as far afield as Australia. The fact that for Buddy it got better still is testament to one of America's great jazz drummers, and given his parents' careers, one of the great showmen of jazz

Buddy was born in New York City in September 1917 and by the time he was eleven he was fronting his own band, although it would be another decade before Buddy made it into a recording studio. In 1936 pianist Joe Bushkin tried to persuade Benny Goodman to take on Buddy, but the Goodman band was a co-operative so there was no way he could dump his man, despite Bushkin saying, "He's the greatest drummer in the world." In early in 1937 Rich began playing drums for Joe Marsala's Septet at the Hickory House in New York. Later, when Marsala went into the studio, they were renamed the Chicagoans to record "Woo Woo" – the first time that Rich was heard on record. While it opens with a bit of a flourish, it gives little hint of what was to come. "Might Like The Blues" was the first song they recorded that day and it is such a pedestrian blues tune that even someone who had never played the drums could probably have pulled it off.

Buddy's next gig was with bandleader Adrian Rollini in early 1938, and he then backed Maxine Sullivan at a session in March, followed by Bunny Berigan at the end of the year. Billed as Bunny Berigan and his Men, Rich played with a young trombonist called Ray Conniff who had been with Bunny for a while. None of the four sides they recorded give any real indication of what Buddy was

Buddy Rich, backstage at the Strand, New York, c. August 1946.

about. In January of 1939 Buddy joined the Artie Shaw Orchestra and stayed with them for most of the year. These were the first recordings on which he was heard in anything like his future glory. On "Serenade To A Savage," there's vintage Buddy Rich, all tom toms and driving beat. Coupled with "Traffic Jam," these sides made people started to take notice of the man behind the kit. Artie Shaw recognized how important Rich was saying, "he made the band almost into a new band overnight." At the same time he helped turn Shaw into one of America's top-earning band leaders, as well as becoming *Downbeat's* No.1 Swing Band in 1939.

In November 1939, Shorty after the outbreak of the Second World War, Buddy got his big break when he joined the Tommy Dorsey Orchestra. But it could have been so different. Artie Shaw had been ill towards the end of the summer and decided to break up his band and quit music for a while. Dorsey snapped up Buddy and he was soon an integral part of the trombonist's band.

Rich quickly settled onto the Dorsey band drum stool, recording four sides on November 24, 1939 including "Losers Weepers," which carries right on from where he left off with Artie Shaw. Rich drives the band ever onwards, as soloist after soloist strut their stuff. Buddy had been in the band barely three months when another new boy turned up – the twenty-four year old former singer with Harry James' band, Frank Sinatra. There's no record of what Frank thought of Tommy's drumming on those first few gigs. However, Dorsey, when introducing Sinatra to Rich, is reported to have said. "I want you to meet another pain in the ass."

Over the next few weeks the band played in Chicago, Indianapolis, Meadowbrook in New Jersey, were in and out of the studio in Chicago and New York, before opening at the Paramount Theater on Times Square at Broadway and 43rd Street on March 13, 1940. The Paramount was billed as the "Home of New York's Greatest 2-for-1 Show." For the price of admission the audience got to see a movie – Bing Crosby and Bob Hope's *The Road To Singapore*, and a whole host of live entertainment. Tommy Dorsey, his Trombone and his Orchestra featuring, in order of billing, Bunny Berigan "World's Hottest Trumpet" (Harry James may well have disputed that); Buddy Rich, at the drums; Frank Sinatra, Baritone, and the Pied Piper Quartette. Also on the bill

"No other drummer has ever matched his rhythmic fire and excitement."
~ Critic George T. Simon

"There's only one genius on this instrument." ~ *Gene Krupa pointing at Buddy Rich*

were Winfield and Ford, Stepping Stars of Harlem and Red Skelton the comedian.

Sinatra ended up sharing a room with, according to the singer, "another loner, Buddy Rich," while they toured. After Dorsey, Buddy was the third big ego in the band, Sinatra being the other; it was a situation that could blow at any moment. One night in June, back stage at the Hotel Astor in New York, things came to something of a head, according to singer Jo Stafford, who was one of the Pied Pipers. "Buddy called Frank a name and Frank grabbed a heavy pitcher filled with water and ice and threw it at Buddy's head. Buddy ducked. If he hadn't he probably would have been killed or seriously hurt. The pitcher hit the wall so hard that pieces of glass were embedded in the plaster." On other occasions their simmering bad feeling boiled over and the "boy-singer" and the bolshie drummer traded punches.

The pianist with the Dorsey band, Joe Bushkin, was another who had regular run-ins with Buddy Rich; Joe might have thought Buddy was the greatest drummer, but that never held him back. One night Bushkin was late for a show, so late that they had already started and when Joe arrived Dorsey stopped the band and said "You used to play with us." Joe was also in the wrong uniform – it was a Tuesday, the day they changed into the light suits, rather than the dark suit he was wearing. Joe was fined the regular forfeit of having to buy the whole band a drink. As the waiter approached with wine for everybody, Joe told him to "cancel the wine." He said he wasn't paying because every night that Tommy was away Buddy Rich had been late and he, Joe, wasn't paying until Buddy paid first. "Afterwards Buddy and I went out in the park and beat the living daylights out of each other; it was a fighting band." Tommy came running out and tried to stop the fight, not because he was worried about two of his star turns. "Take the jackets off," he said, "we got another program to play."

Rich left Dorsey in 1942 when he joined the Marines but was back with his old boss by 1944, although it wasn't long before he had the urge to break out on his own. From 1945 until the early 1950s Buddy led his own band which he sometimes conducted from out front with another drummer sitting in for the man himself; he also took to singing a bit, having been encouraged by none other than Sinatra himself. He appeared with the Jazz at

BR
BR
BR
BR
BR
BR

the Philharmonic band, and then in 1953 he joined Harry James' band. He left for a spell to play with Tommy Dorsey again from 1954 to 1955, after which he returned to Harry James where he stayed until the early sixties.

For several years Rich, like anyone who was playing jazz, struggled with the onslaught of the beat boom, but in 1966, much against the odds, Buddy started a new pile-driving big band. It was, to all intents and purposes, a traditional big band, but with Rich at the helm it had show-stopping ensemble playing, punctuated with Rich's dynamic solos. Pretty quickly the Buddy Rich Big Band was playing venues in Los Angeles and Las Vegas, and went back in the studio, recording for Pacific Jazz, as well as being captured on live albums.

One track in particular helped to revitalize Buddy's reputation, the stunning medley from *West Side Story* that the band performed on the album *Buddy Rich's Swingin' New Big Band*. It was so complex that few other drummers or bands would have attempted it. The band also backed Sammy Davis Jr on an album recorded in Las Vegas, which seemed to turn back the clock to an era when big band jazz was cool, proving that it was finally hip to be square.

The big band stayed together until 1974 when Buddy broke it up and went back to a small group format, appearing regularly at his own club, Buddy's Place, in New York City. Even then, he still dusted off the big band for short tours, and remained very popular in Europe. A DVD of a performance in Holland has recently been released that includes "Channel One Suite" with its climactic Rich solo. He was sixty-one when this was recorded, which makes the power and dexterity of his playing even more remarkable; he had already played his way though most of the demanding set. In the 1980s Buddy once again broke the rules and brought back his big band, this time with a

The Buddy Rich Band: Buddy Rich, Stanley Fishelson, Tommy Allison, Phil Gilbert, Bill Howell, Mario Daone, Bob Ascher, Chunky Koenigsberg, Eddie Caine, Jerry Thirkeld, Allen Eager, Mickey Rich, Harvey Levine, H. (Harvey) Leonard, Gene Dell, Tubby Phillips, and Kay Stanley.

"He was emotional, tender, angry, and most of all a perfectionist and consummate artist." ~ *Cathy Rich, Buddy's daughter*

whole group of younger musicians. While he still had the ability to be the extrovert he also demonstrated why he was such a great drummer. He had the expertise to play like a metronome, never getting off the beat, while showing that there was great skill and beauty in simplicity.

Among the awards that Buddy received were, the *Downbeat* magazine Hall of Fame Award – he's been the winner of the *Downbeat* magazine Readers' Poll on many occasions; there have been three Grammy nomination; he played at the inauguration of Franklin D. Roosevelt as well as for Presidents Reagan and John F. Kennedy.

Buddy's temper was legendary, to the extent that there were numerous tapes in circulation of him letting rip in the recording studio when something didn't quite come up to his idea of perfection. On one occasion he even fired a member of his band for having a beard. He was also very funny and maintained a long-running gag about how he disliked the Osmond brothers, especially Donny, and their music. He wore a Donny Osmond badge in his lapel right up until his final television appearance on a British talk show just a couple of weeks before he died.

Buddy Rich went into hospital for surgery on a brain tumour in March 1987, and when he was asked if there was anything he was allergic to, he quickly fired back, "Country music." He died on April 2, 1987 from complications arising from surgery; he was seventy and had worked during every decade of his life.

Buddy Rich at the Arcadia Ballroom, New York, c. May 1947.

BUDDY RICH

BORN September 30, 1917 in New York, NY

DIED April 2, 1987 in Los Angeles, CA

INSTRUMENT Drums

FIRST RECORDED 1937

INFLUENCES Chick Webb, Dave Tough Jo Jones

RECOMMENDED LISTENING

This One's For Basie *(1956)*

Driver *(1960)*

Rich in London *(1971)*

Jazz Icons - Buddy Rich Live in '78 DVD *(2006)*

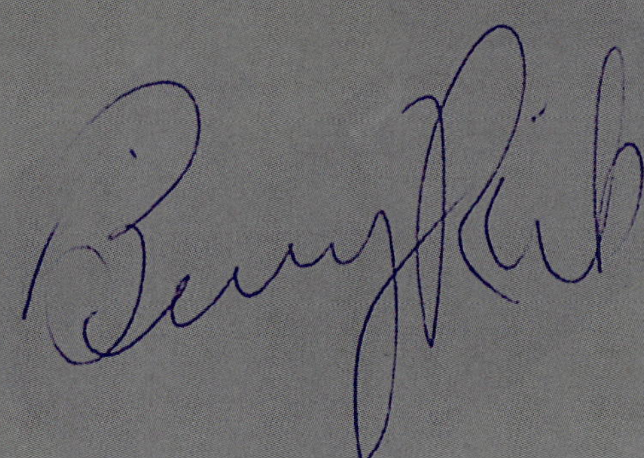

WOODLEY

Dizzy Gillespie

"It's possible people might know me and not know my music. But once I let my jaws go, the world knows."
~ Dizzy Gillespie, 1987

He was crazy, unpredictable, brash, extrovert, and stylish, as well as being a trumpet virtuoso, which all helped to make Dizzy Gillespie an icon of jazz and an inspiration to many younger trumpeters. When Dizzy's bop first came along, someone coined the phrase, "be hip, be sharp, be bop!" It says a lot about the dizzy heights to which he aspired and more importantly attained. He may have been the "Clown Prince of Jazz," but without him jazz would certainly have been a lot less interesting.

John Birks Gillespie was born in South Carolina, the youngest of nine children; his father was a bricklayer who struggled to cope financially, like many poor black families in the South. By all accounts young John suffered at the hands of his father on numerous occasions, and beatings were a feature of his early life. While his father's harsh treatment stayed with him for the rest of his life, so did the fact that he was a keen musician who played in a part-time band and stored many of the band's instruments at his home. By the time John was ten-years old, when his father died, he had played a little on all of them. Fortunately, a teacher at school continued to encourage his interest and he took up the cornet.

In 1932 John went to Laurinburg Institute in North Carolina because they needed a trumpet player for their band and, at fifteen, he was already a talented player. He also learned the piano and got to grips with harmony and the structure of music. His cousin, a trombone player, was also a pupil and the two teenagers encouraged each other's musical exploration. In 1935 the Gillespie family moved to Philadelphia, preventing him from graduating. As soon as he arrived, however, he was playing with bands in the city's Southside clubs.

Gillespie soon found himself in the Frankie Fairfax Band, Phillie's finest at the time. Among the other musicians in the band was pianist Bill Doggett, who together with trumpeter Charlie Shavers helped to make the band popular; both also helped John. Doggett worked with him on mastering arranging, while Shavers taught him many of the solos made famous by Roy Eldridge. While he was intent on learning, he was also keen on playing the fool and having a good time. It was while he was with the

Dizzy Gillespie, New York, c. May 1947.

"He was about as crazy as a fox." ~ A fellow musician from his big band days

Fairfax band that he became "Dizzy."

After two years in Philadelphia, Dizzy headed east to New York, increasingly the jazz capital of America, the place where things happened. He had been promised a job with Lucky Millender's band, but at the eleventh hour it fell through. Dizzy eventually secured a place in Teddy Hill's band in late April 1937, and the following month he was in the studio recording half a dozen sides.

No sooner had they finished than the band headed across the Atlantic to tour England and France for several months. For Dizzy, the trip was an eye-opener; for musicians, jazz fans and audiences throughout Britain it was a treat to see a real American big band. Dizzy was obviously still learning his craft, which is perhaps why he did not record with French jazz legend Django Reinhardt, along with many others from the Hill band in July. Then again it might have been, as others have suggested, that Dizzy was not the most popular band member on account of the high interest he charged his band mates in a money-lending racket.

Back in America, Dizzy worked with Alberto Socarras' Orchestra and Al Cooper's Savoy Sultans. After another spell with the Teddy Hill Band, Dizzy hit the relative big time in August 1939, landing a job with Cab Calloway's band. Around the same time he did a session with Lionel Hampton, and among those he worked with were Benny Carter, Coleman Hawkins, Ben Webster, Charlie Christian, the brilliant guitarist, as well as Calloway's bassist Milt Hinton. "Hot Mallets" from this session is the first time Dizzy can be heard prominently, on a record. Callaway, like every big band leader, was keen to keep his boys on the road and it was while they were touring in Kansas City in 1940 that Dizzy met and jammed with Charlie Parker for the first time.

Back in New York, Dizzy spent much of his free time in 1941, when not working with Calloway, jamming with Thelonious Monk, Kenny Clarke and Charlie Parker. Dizzy would play at Minton's on a regular basis, developing his style and honing his playing. Dizzy's love of a good time did nothing to endear him to Cab Callaway, who didn't take kindly to his trumpeter's antics. The bandleader angered Dizzy by hiring another trumpeter, named Jonah Jones, who then got most of the featured solos.

One day in the autumn of 1941 Jones flicked a paper "spitball" across the bandstand hitting Cab Calloway in the process. Without a thought he turned on the usual suspect. Dizzy, for once innocent, drew a knife on his boss, which cut him. Dizzy was fired instantly. From then

"(I was) looking for a way to emphasize the more beautiful notes in swing. When you hum it, you just naturally say 'bebop, be-de-bop.' "
~ Dizzy Gillespie, 1946

on, Gillespie became something of a musical mercenary working with artists that included Ella Fitzgerald, Coleman Hawkins, Benny Carter, Charlie Barnet, Earl Hines, Woody Herman and Duke Ellington to name just a few.

Dizzy, finally, played with Lucky Millinder's outfit and it was with them in July 1942 that he recorded "Little John Special," his first real bop solo, although this was within the context of a big band in full swing. Gillespie also worked with his own group, but after meeting Billy Eckstine, while they were both working with Earl Hines, Gillespie joined the singer's new band in 1944 as musical director. Dizzy's first session with his new boss was in December, and among the others in the band were tenor saxophonists, Gene Ammons and Dexter Gordon, drummer Art Blakey, with Tadd Dameron as their arranger. On this first session a very young and timid girl singer sang several songs. The problem with these sessions was that they were badly engineered and then the recordings were badly pressed; Dizzy and many others soon left.

In 1945 Dizzy worked with his own group, as well as the Boyd Raeburn Orchestra. He also did some sessions with Sarah Vaughan, including a version of "Lover Man," featuring Charlie Parker, on which Sarah shines. In November he recorded for the first time with Miles Davis in Charlie Parker's ReBoppers at a studio on New York's Broadway. Early in 1946 he appeared at *Jazz at the Philharmonic* and recorded a number of sessions with various small groups that he led.

Having tried unsuccessfully in 1945 to get a big band off the ground, Dizzy succeeded in the late spring of 1946 taking it on the road to venues that included Washington's Spotlight Lounge. The orchestra featured among its stars, Sonny Stitt, on alto sax, Thelonious Monk on piano and Kenny Clarke on drums; Dizzy himself handled the vocals. By 1947 Dizzy was dabbling with Afro-Cuban jazz and introduced conga player, Chano Pozo and Lorenzo Salan, a bongo player into the orchestra's line-up. Through the band in 1947 went Ray Brown on bass, Milt Jackson on vibes and John Lewis on piano, and Kenny Clarke who went on to form the Modern Jazz Quartet.

By 1950 the difficulties, both financial and managerial, of keeping a big band together began to take its toll and Dizzy gave up his own orchestra, joining Stan Kenton for a short while as featured soloist. He also played and recorded in small group settings that

"If it doesn't hurt your ears it isn't dissonance. But then, I'm a little deaf myself."
~ Dizzy Gillespie, 1948

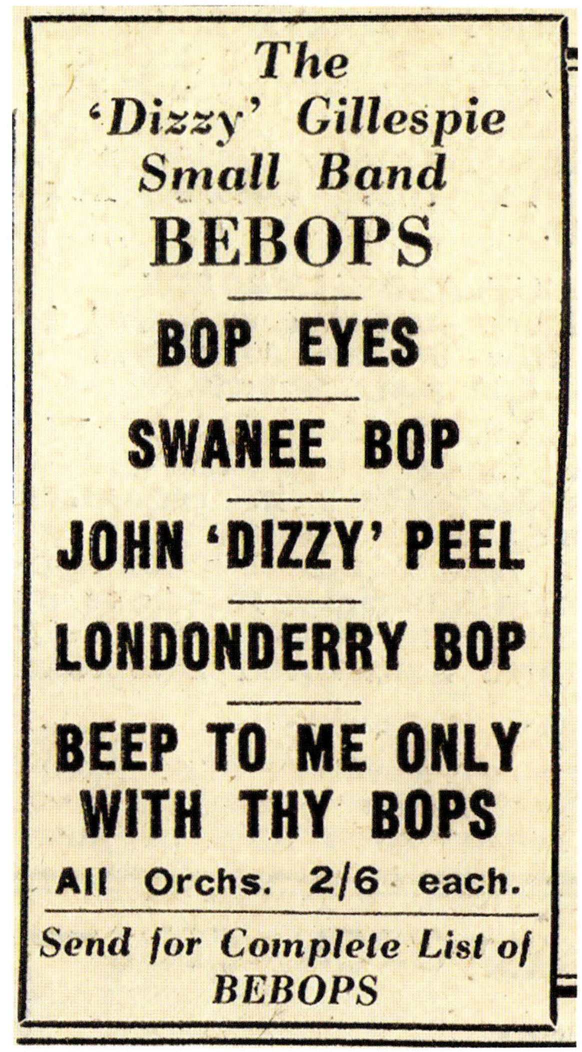

"The style of our music is based on the way that he (Charlie Parker) played. I had something to do with the harmony and the rhythmic sense. Monk created the harmony and (drummer) Kenny Clarke created the rhythm to go with it. We developed all of that to go with the music."
~ Dizzy Gillespie

included the Dizzy Gillespie, Charlie Parker Quintet which also featured, Thelonious Monk, bassist, Curly Russell and Buddy Rich on drums.

For the most part during the early 1950s the small group setting was Dizzy's chosen recording platform. The people he played with during this period, either in his own groups or those of others, reads like the who's who of jazz. Besides Parker, Davis and Monk, there was John Coltrane, Art Blakey, J.J. Jackson, Kenny Burrell, Bud Powell, Don Byas, Charles Mingus, Oscar Peterson, Illinois Jacquet and Stan Getz. Having worked in France in 1948, and been a big hit, he went back several times during the first three years of the decade where his work continued to be well received.

In 1954 he briefly resurrected his orchestra and among

Dizzy Gillespie, New York c. May 1947.

DIZZY GILLESPIE

BORN October 21, 1917 in Cheraw, SC

DIED January 6, 1993 in Yonkers, NY

INSTRUMENT Trumpet

FIRST RECORDED 1937

INFLUENCES Roy Eldridge, Charlie Shavers

RECOMMENDED LISTENING

Diz and Getz *(1953)*

Roy and Diz (Roy Eldridge and Dizzy Gillespie) *(1954)*

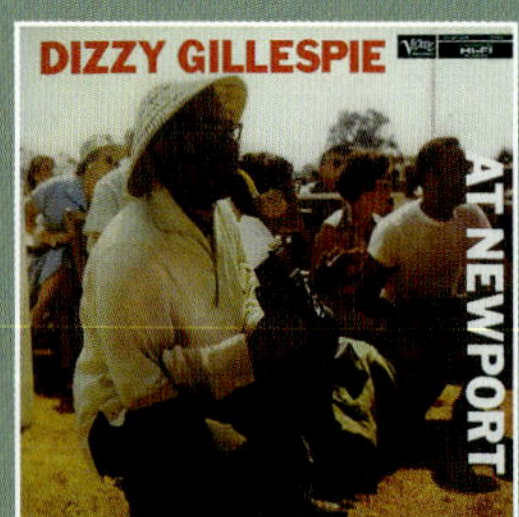

Dizzy Gillespie at Newport (Live) *(1957)*

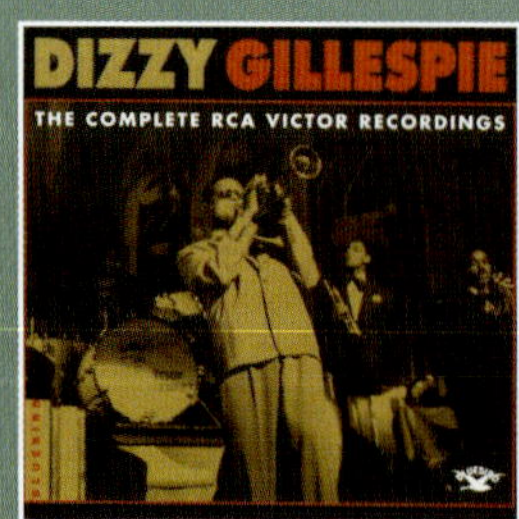

The Complete RCA Recordings 1947-1949 *(1995)*

the trumpet players was twenty-one-year-old Quincy Jones. By this time Dizzy was playing his now famous bent trumpet. The year before someone had accidentally fallen on his trumpet while it was sitting on a stand. It bent the bell so it was pointing upwards in a 45-degree angle. Gillespie liked the sound, so that's the way his trumpets remained. At least, that's the official story; it has been suggested that Dizzy may have seen an English trumpeter with a bent horn in 1937 when he toured with the Teddy Hill Orchestra.

Dizzy's orchestra was another a short-lived affair and he was once again playing with what seemed liked everybody in the jazz world. In 1956 he put the orchestra back together, with Quincy Jones as its musical arranger, and they toured in the Middle East, Eastern Europe, and South America sponsored by the US State Department. In the autumn of 1956 he recorded with his old trumpet hero, Roy Eldridge for the Verve label. The big band stayed together for two years, but after government funding ran out he closed it down to return to the small group format.

From the 1960s onwards Dizzy continued to perform with his Sextet and Quintet as well as guesting on many other projects. In 1971-72 he appeared with the Giants of Jazz, featuring Kai Winding, the trombonist, Sonny Stitt, Thelonious Monk, Al McKibbon on bass and Art Blakey. He also appeared with Charles Mingus' Orchestra, Billy Eckstine, Oscar Peterson, Benny Carter and numerous others. However his days as a cutting edge player had passed and he had settled into a mellower role, although he still loved to joke and play pranks. He even featured on the cruise ships where his humour went over well and his position, as an elder statesman of jazz was secure.

Dizzy died from cancer in January 1993, having helped to change the face of jazz trumpet playing and the face of jazz itself.

Dizzy Gillespie, 52nd Street, New York between 1946 and 1948.

AMERICAS
W. 52 ST.
W 52
AMERICAS
NO PARKING
IN THIS BLOCK
8 A.M. TO 6 P.M.
MON. TO FRI. INCLU
PARKING LIMIT
OTHER TIMES-ONE HOUR
POLICE
DEPT.

ERROLL GARNER

"It's a gift. The good Lord gave it to me and I'm trying to develop it." *~ Erroll Garner, 1951*

Erroll Garner's playing was a joy to hear, filled with exuberance, melody, and a lightness of touch that made his music easy to listen to without it ever being easy listening. He was nicknamed "the Elf," in part because of his size, but also because he played music that was full of humor with a breeziness that made people feel good when they listened. He once said that he just wanted "to get that listener's foot tapping." He usually succeeded.

Erroll Garner was born in Pittsburgh in 1921 and started playing the piano when he was three, playing by ear music he heard from records. His older brother Linton also played piano and later appeared with Fletcher Henderson and with singer Billy Eckstine's Band. At seven, he turned pro, playing piano with an outfit called the Kan-De Kids on KDKA, a Pittsburgh radio station. By his teenage years he was playing with more experienced musicians and it soon became evident that Erroll was not someone who fitted into a rigid group structure with ensemble playing; his style always made him stand out.

Erroll began working in Pittsburgh's entertainment district at nightclubs that included the Ritz Café. Art Tatum had the regular slot at the Ritz. A few years older than Garner, one night when his young rival played in the club, the manager made Tatum, no mean pianist himself, switch to drums, because Erroll was so much better. Even Tatum agreed. "The cat not only played it, but he added his own dressings." Later that year Erroll, who was still only sixteen, joined saxophonist Leroy Brown's band, and stayed for three years before heading to New York in early 1941. He went to back a singer who became so annoyed that Garner was better than she was that she fired him; Erroll got a job in a club in New Jersey instead.

Garner went back to Pittsburgh for a while and played in various clubs, as well as working with Billy Eckstine. He amazed the singer by always being able to just play along with whatever he sang, whether or not he had ever heard the song before. By 1944 he moved to New York permanently and worked in various nightclubs. He met up with his old sparring partner Art Tatum and substituted for him in his trio when he was ill; later, after Tatum left, Erroll took over when it became known as the Slam Stewart Trio.

By 1946 Garner was leading his own trio and quickly proved to be a big hit with the audiences in the clubs on 52nd Street. He always felt most comfortable in the trio format and that's the way he played for the rest of his

Erroll Garner playing in New York.

"Three's a crowd, three's enough." ~ Erroll Garner

career, other than the odd foray as a soloist. He went to Los Angeles in 1947, where he recorded with Charlie Parker, playing on the "Cool Blues" sessions.

Much of what made Garner's playing so different was that his arrangements had the sound of a big band, even though it was just a trio that was playing Erroll's unique musical settings. Perhaps more amazing is the fact that they were purely in his head, having been "composed" by Garner drawing on his love of big bands – Duke Ellington and Count Basie in particular. It was Basie's guitarist ,Freddie Green, whose playing provided the inspiration to his steady rhythmic guitar-like left hand. This, coupled with his way of playing slightly behind the beat, which some have likened to Billie Holiday's singing, produced more than just jazz piano – it was jazz piano with soul.

Garner was honored in France for his recording with Charlie Parker, and as a result was invited to appear at the Paris Jazz Festival in 1948. Garner was greeted with huge acclaim, which staggered him as he had no idea of his fame outside America; to be fair he was probably a lot less well known in America at this point in his career. Back in New York in 1949 Garner played at many clubs but he especially enjoyed playing at a new club – "Manhattan's midtown mecca of jive… Birdland."

Garner was beginning to be acknowledged in America as someone who had the ability to cross over from purely jazz audiences to fans of increasingly sophisticated forms of popular music. Having recorded for a whole bunch of smaller labels, he was signed to Columbia Records who had the muscle to elevate Garner to a whole new audience. This was particularly so because they were a pioneer in the LP format.

Columbia had launched the $33^1/_3$-rpm long-playing record on the June 21, 1948 at the Waldorf Hotel. While there was great secrecy surrounding the launch, Columbia had over 100 titles ready to release by July 1. At their Dealer Conference in Atlantic City on June 21, a company executive gave a speech while an LP of Tchaikovsky's *Nutcracker Suite* played. All the delegates could see it playing via a large mirror suspended above the turntable. At the end of the 18-minute side, (more than 4 times longer than an existing 78-rpm record) the crowd gave a standing ovation! Within a year, one million American homes had the equipment they needed to play LPs, and the revolutions' revolution had begun. Long playing records were sold at $4.95 each and to encourage sales of the necessary turntables, on which to play them, a Philco player was for sale costing $29.25 along with three free LPs – a neat piece of marketing.

By 1951 Garner was earning $100,000 a year ($1.5 million today), and had a Manhattan apartment, as well as a house in suburban White Plains. He had been helped

"I just play what I feel. Suddenly I hit a groove that moves me, and then I take off. I don't worry about how it'll come out." ~ *Erroll Garner*

Erroll Garner playing in New York.

in all this by a new manager he had acquired a couple of years earlier. Martha Glaser was his only ever manager and Erroll, her only client.

It wasn't just the clubs that he was playing by this time; there were concert halls, tours and television, which greatly increased his exposure and, in turn, the sales of his albums. In 1952 Garner undertook a tour that started out in Birdland before heading steadily west; they even played in Hawaii. It was a master class of piano by four master pianists. There was Meade Lux Lewis and Pete Johnson who faced each other across two grand pianos. Lewis pounded out "Honky Tonk Train Blues," and Johnson played classic thirties numbers, including "Roll 'em Pete," along with other boogie-woogie classics. Tatum, the master pianist from the swing era, played beautifully, but it was Garner who stole the show. He sounded so modern compared to the boogie-woogie of Johnson and Lewis, but he also made Tatum sound dated. As one report said, "He treated happy Birdlanders to big, chunky chords crammed full of notes, then showed them how he could switch to rainbows of glassy melody and fantasy."

In 1954 he recorded "Misty," which became synonymous with Garner for the rest of his career. He wrote the song, so he said, "While watching a rainbow from an aircraft window." Johnny Burke added lyrics to it later and it was turned into a chart hit by Johnny Mathis. In 1971 it was pivotal to the storyline of Clint Eastwood's film *Play Misty For Me.*

In the September of the following year Garner appeared at a concert in Carmel, California that was recorded and became a seminal jazz album, selling in huge quantities. *The Concert By The Sea,* as the album is called, features his new bassist Eddie Calhoun and drummer Denzil Best, who had only just joined Garner, in a program of material that redefined jazz piano. People who had said they didn't like jazz suddenly found they did. From the opening "I'll Remember April" and in particular the second track on the album, "Teach Me Tonight," it heralds a new kind of jazz standard. In 1957 he recorded another big-selling album for Columbia, it was also the first time he recorded with strings. Called *Other Voices,* it featured "Misty" as its opening track.

"I like to play certain tunes because of their melody. Why should I disguise that melody? Musicians today just aren't getting along with the people. They forget they are people themselves, they can't be artistic hermits." *~ Erroll Garner*

"Erroll Garner became my 'forever jazz piano idol' after I heard his amazing Concert By The Sea in 1957. Take a listen to his 'Teach Me Tonight' track... perfect!" ~ *Bruce Johnston of the Beach Boys*

A couple of years later Erroll had a protracted falling out with Columbia Records, who didn't think he was recording enough material for which they certainly had the demand from the fans. It ended up in court and both sides eventually settled out of court, allowing Garner to record for his own company, which in turn, leased the recordings to whichever label suited him and his manager to do business with – a novel scheme that was later copied by numerous rock and pop artists.

Live work always played a big part in Garner's career, and as the sixties rolled around he seemed to be working constantly. One aspect of his concerts that delighted audiences, and at times confused his musicians, was his enormous repertoire, coupled with the fact that he seemed able to play whatever song he chose to, in any key of his choosing. Once when he was asked about this he said. "I play 'Misty' a thousand times a year and each time I like to add a little something.

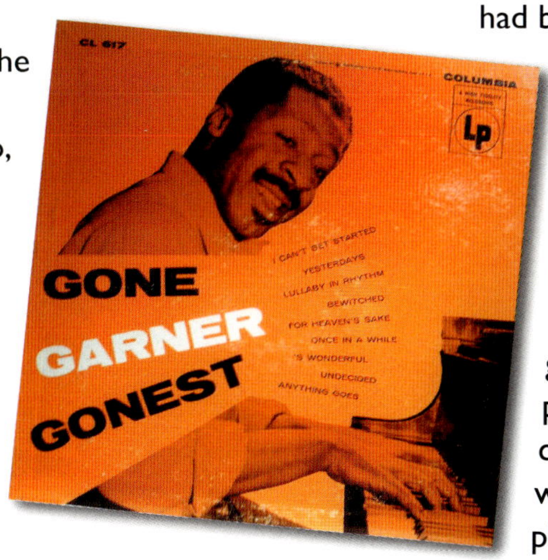

Erroll kept on working well into the 1970s. He re-recorded "Misty" yet again for the soundtrack of Clint Eastwood's film in 1971, as well as recording more albums. He also kept up a hectic schedule of live work, but his health was failing. He had been told to quit smoking as he had emphysema, but he failed to heed the warnings. Eventually in February 1975 he caught viral pneumonia and spent time in hospital in Chicago. They discovered he had lung cancer and he never appeared in public again. Errol Garner died in January 1977 aged just fifty-five.

Although only five-feet, two-inches tall, he was a giant of the jazz piano, doing more to introduce people to jazz than almost any single one of his contemporaries. Despite his height, he was blessed with hands that had a huge stretch. It enabled him to play things that others couldn't. He never did learn to

Concert program for the 1963 British tour.

read music and trusted his ears, allowing him to play music with a natural swing and sway. He amazed audiences by being able to play stunning and complex runs on the piano without ever looking at his hands. But it was his musical mind that was truly amazing. His seemingly limitless repertoire, his inventiveness, coupled with his love of music, made him unique. We are unlikely ever to be lucky enough to have another like Erroll Garner among us.

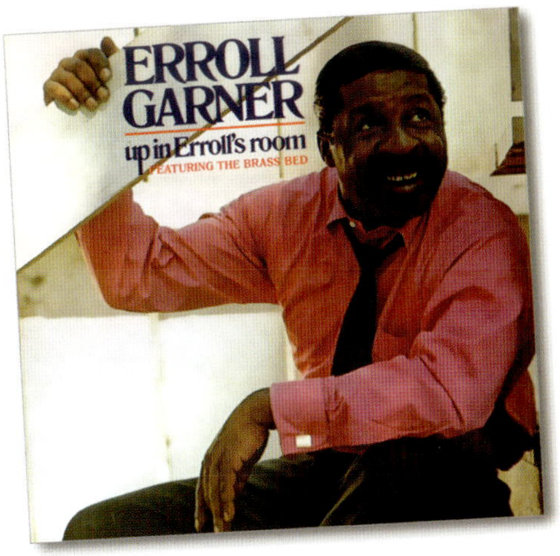

Erroll Garner playing in New York.

ERROLL GARNER

BORN June 15, 1921 in Pittsburgh, PA

DIED January 2, 1977 in New Jersey, NJ

INSTRUMENT Piano

FIRST RECORDED 1944

INFLUENCES Zez Confrey, Earl Hines

RECOMMENDED LISTENING

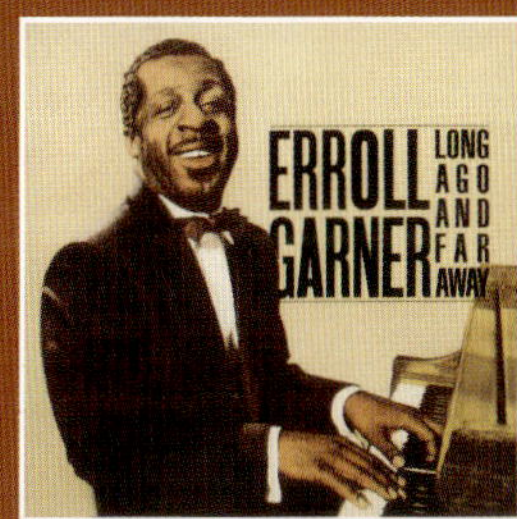

***Long Ago And Far Away** (1950)*

***Body And Soul** (1951)*

***Concert By The Sea** (1955)*

***Solo Flight** (1952)*

NOT
ANY MUSICAL
MUSIC OR
LEFT IN
CARNEGIE

Charlie Parker

"I think all the guys like Bird and Dizzy contributed so much to making the steps of progress of modern music. Those guys had wonderful minds." *~ Count Basie*

"Bird," as he was known, was one of the most important figures in the development of jazz, and in particular the development of bop. His was a thoughtful kind of jazz, but not constricted by arrangements, for he was the master of improvisation. A troubled man, with drugs and drink at the heart of his problems, he was also a genius. He is one man of which it can be said without fear of contradiction, that he changed the course of jazz history.

Charles Parker Jr was another who hailed from the early 20th century jazz well that was Kansas City. He was born in August 1920 to a teenage mother, and his father had once worked in a travelling minstrel show. By all accounts he had a pretty good childhood, although his father was more interested in gambling than parenting. When he was twelve his family moved to an area of Kansas City close to the jazz district.

By the time he was fourteen, his father had left, leaving his doting mother to bring up Charlie. He was besotted with music and the life of the musicians he saw around 12th Street and Vine. Eventually, after a lot of persuasion from her son and a lot of overtime for her (she was an office cleaner), Charlie's mother bought him a beaten up second-hand alto sax.

By the time he was sixteen Charlie was married but it did not curtail his musical ambitions. Charlie played wherever he could in Kansas City, but he also watched and learned from many bands: Mary Lou Williams, Basie, Pete Johnson, Buster Moten and Lester Young, who he especially loved.

Young Charlie tried jamming and improvising. Some of his initial attempts on "Honeysuckle Rose" or "Lazy River" were not too bad, but on one occasion he attempted to play "Body and Soul" in double tempo. It was a disaster. According to Parker., "I went home and cried and didn't play again for three months." He also tried jamming with some of Count Basie's band, but this too ended in humiliation, when Jo Jones, Basie's drummer, dropped his cymbal on the floor to denote that the jam was over, and young Charlie was rubbish; Bird held a grudge against the Basie band forever more.

It was probably in the summer of 1937 that he got a permanent job at a holiday resort in the Ozark Mountains

Charlie Parker, Carnegie Hall, New York, c. 1946.

"Music is your own experience, your own thoughts, your wisdom. If you don't live it, it won't come out of your horn." ~ Charlie Parker

where at last he began to master the rudiments of proper playing. The pianist with the band taught him about harmony, and Charlie listened endlessly to records to dissect the solos and learn them off by heart. Having got inside the music's DNA, he was then able to break free and become a brilliant improviser. He learned more back in Kansas City, where he became a protégé of the more experienced Buster Smith

In late 1938 or early 1939 Parker, arrived in Chicago. Like many of the clubs in the city, the 65 Club held a breakfast dance in the early hours., where musicians from all over town would end up to hang out. A four-piece was playing, and according to singer Billy Eckstine, "A guy comes up that looks like he just got off a freight car – the raggedest guy. He asks Goon Gardner (the alto sax player), 'Say man can I come up and blow your horn'" Goon was more interested in talking to the women at the bar, so he just handed over his sax. According to Eckstine, "He blew the hell out of that thing. It was Charlie Parker, just come in from Kansas City." He was eighteen.

In 1940 Parker, who was by now separated from his wife and seriously imbibing drugs and drink of all types, joined pianist Jay McShann's band. Bird was a complete contradiction; he took his music so seriously, but every other aspect of his life was out of control. He started writing arrangements for the band, as well as leading the sax section. The first time that anyone outside of a club heard Charlie blow his horn was in November 1940, when the McShann Combo was heard on KFBI, a Wichita radio station.

Six months later Parker was in a Dallas recording studio working with McShann for a Decca session. As well as playing alto, Charlie arranged "Hootie Blues." In November the McShann Quartet recorded some more sides, while the Orchestra recorded a couple of shows for the American Forces Radio Service. It was during this time that Charlie picked up the nickname "Yardbird,"but no one can remember quite why. Before long everyone just called him "Bird."

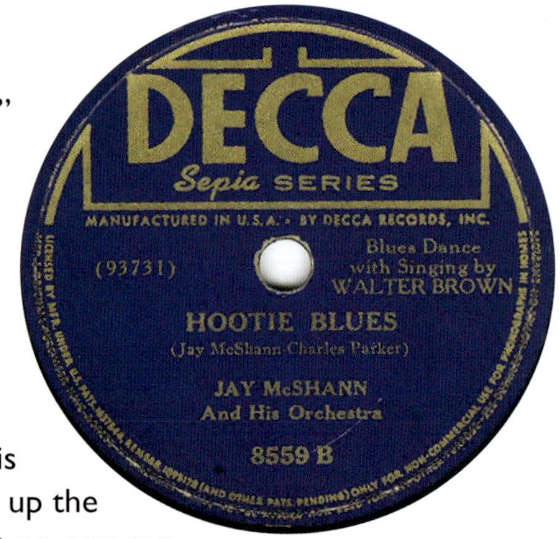

The McShann band were at the Savoy Ballroom in January 1942, which is when Charlie first began to get serious recognition from other musicians, especially at

"Charlie had a photographic mind. When we would rehearse a new arrangement, he would run his part down once and when we were ready to play it a second time, he knew the whole thing from memory." ~ Earl Hines

"I spent my first week in New York looking for Bird and Dizzy. Man, I went everywhere looking for those cats." *~ Miles Davis*

after-show sessions at Monroe's Uptown House. Not that everyone "got" what Parker was up to. There was none of the smoothness of regular swing bands in what Charlie played; many just heard it as notes in some random order. Parker's music was challenging for many people and incomprehensible to many others.

In 1943 Parker played in Earl Hines' band, along with Dizzy Gillespie and Benny Green. Hines recalls how conscientious they all were. "They would carry exercise books with them and would go through the books in the dressing rooms when we played theaters." It was with Hines' band that Parker began playing the tenor sax. It was a case of necessity being the mother of invention, as Budd Johnson had left Hines and so a tenor player was required. At first Parker couldn't get used to his new sax. "Man this thing is too big." The problem according to Charlie was he couldn't "feel" it. There was another problem – Charlie was really unreliable. According to Billy Eckstine, he missed nearly as many shows as he did; in the end, the other musicians shamed him into improving, helped by the fact that he took to sleeping in the theater.

Eventually the Hines band broke up, and Parker played with both Andy Kirk and Noble Sissle's bands for brief spells; he also moved to Chicago, which is where Billy Eckstine found him, and got him into his band. They started rehearsing in St Louis and worked on numbers such as "Cool Breeze" and "Lady Bird," which Tadd Dameron arranged.

Parker's sojourn with Bill's band didn't last long and by late 1944 he was once again on his own, although he spent most of his time with Dizzy Gillespie playing up and down 52nd Street. This was the genesis of be-bop, a term whose origins are shrouded in mystery. Recording was impossible until September 1944, as the Musicians' Union had a ban in force. It was around this time that Parker first met Miles Davis, with whom he had an uneasy, but very fruitful relationship.

By 1945 Parker and Gillespie's band were in demand by those in the jazz-know and in early 1946 they had gone on tour to California, but Bird was up to his old unreliable ways, disappearing when he was supposed to be playing, and making Dizzy's on-stage life very challenging. Dizzy just managed around the problem by taking vibraphonist Milt Jackson with them to deputise for Charlie when he went AWOL. As well as the six-week booking at Billy Berg's, they played Jazz at the Philharmonic in a band that included Lester Young. In true Parker fashion, he arrived late for the gig at the Philharmonic Auditorium. He walked in during the piano solo and Gillespie asked, "Where you been?" Parker let his sax do the talking.

When the six-week booking in Los Angeles finished, Dizzy headed back east while Parker stayed in California. Soon West Coast bop fans were seeking out Charlie; a hip record-shop owner named Ross Russell decided there was an opportunity and approached Parker with an offer of a recording contract with the label he proposed to set up. The first Dial Record session was in February

"They teach you there's a boundary line to music. But, man, there's no boundary line to art." ~ *Charlie Parker*

1946, and despite Charlie's heroin problems, it went well.

The next session was in March, when they recorded "Yardbird Suite" and "A Night in Tunisia." Parker had assembled a septet that included Miles Davis, Lucky Thompson and Dodo Marmarosa. Despite Parker hovering on the cusp of a disaster, this was a pivotal moment in modern jazz. By the next session in July his supplier had been arrested and with no heroin, Parker was drinking gin by the bucketful in a vain attempt to compensate for the lack of drugs. Bird was barely able to play, and listening to "Lover Man" with Charlie struggling is desperately sad.

Parker spent six months at Camarillo State Mental Hospital, but by February 1947 he was back in the studio sounding better than ever. He recorded "Relaxing at Camarillo," "Stupendous," "Cool Blues" – with Erroll Garner on piano, and "Bird's Nest." These sides are arguably the cornerstones of the Parker legend. As well as sounding great, Parker was looking fitter, and after he finished in Los Angeles he went back to New York.

Back on the East Coast, he formed a new quartet with Miles Davis, Duke Jordan, Tommy Potter and Max Roach. Parker lost no time in getting back into the studio and recorded some more great sides in the autumn of 1947 that included "Bird of Paradise," "Bird Feathers," and "Scrapple From The Apple." More sessions followed, producing a string of brilliant recordings that were augmented with performances around town, including a concert at Carnegie Hall with Dizzy.

In December 1949 a new club opened in New York, named Birdland in the saxophonist's honor. This was followed by a visit to Europe, and Parker at last seemed to be getting his life under control, even if the drugs and booze were never entirely absent from his life. Parker's band was great around this time, featuring a young John Coltrane and wowing audiences on both sides of the Atlantic.

Charlie Parker and Miles Davis at the Three Deuces, New York, c. August 1947.

In 1950 he began living with a dancer named Chan Richardson, despite only having married his long-term girlfriend Doris two years earlier. Charlie and Chan had a daughter in 1951 and a son in 1952. Sadly Charlie's daughter died from pneumonia in 1954, an event that brought on the final decline of a man whose mind was fragile from self-abuse. Things got so bad that he was even banned from Birdland. By September 1954 Bird had a breakdown and also attempted suicide. After a spell in hospital, he did get back on his feet and was booked to appear at Birdland in March 1955. Before he could fulfill his engagement he died at the home of Baroness Pannonica de Koenigswarter, where Thelonious Monk would also die nearly twenty-seven years later.

Bird was thirty-four when he died, but according to the autopsy report, he had the body of a man over fifty. Lived fast, died young? He certainly lived way too hard, but he helped make modern jazz sound the way it does today.

Dizzy Gillespie and Charlie Parker, Carnegie Hall, New York, c. October 1947.

CHARLIE PARKER

BORN August 29, 1920 in Kansas City, KS

DIED March 12, 1955 in New York, NY

INSTRUMENT Saxophone

FIRST RECORDED 1941

INFLUENCES Walter Knight, Buster Smith

RECOMMENDED LISTENING

Bird and Pres Live *(1946)*

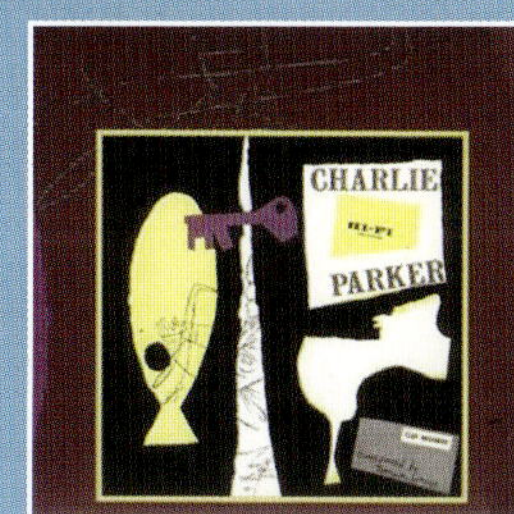

Charlie Parker *(1947)*

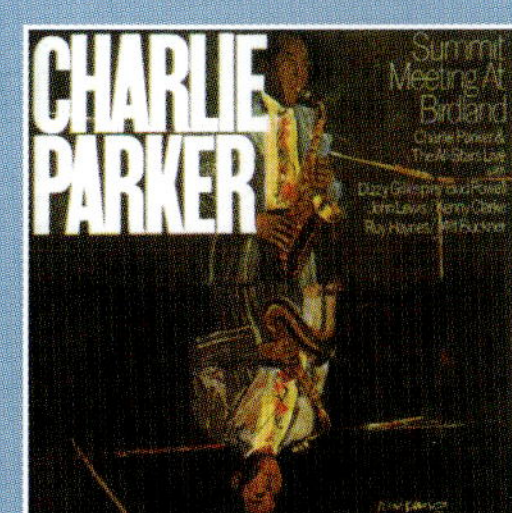

Summit Meeting in Birdland *(19510*

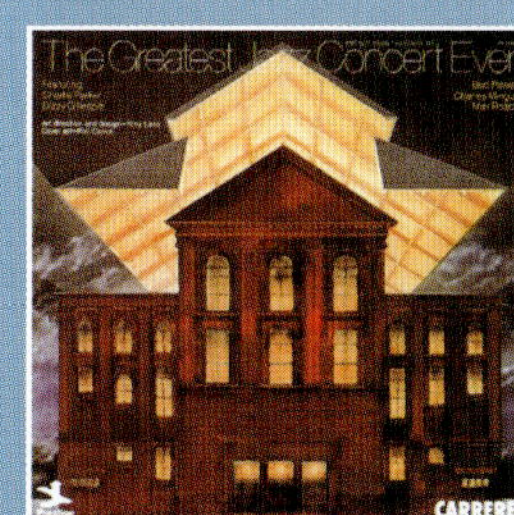

The Greatest Jazz Concert Ever (Live) *(1953)*

ILLINOIS JACQUET

"There are a lot of headaches associated with being a bandleader: dealing with members who are tardy, meeting the payroll, and so on, but if you love the music, it's worth it. I figure that I might as well have headaches and be happy. Because you're going to get headaches, anyhow." *~ Illinois Jacquet*

Illinois Jacquet was one of the links between rhythm and blues, rock'n'roll, and jazz. But it would be all too easy to write him off as a man with a "honking horn" and little else. He worked with many of the best in the jazz business and while his hard reeds were often to the fore, he never lost sight of the fact that he was an entertainer as well as a musician. He was a sensitive ballad player, who played with great subtlety, and lived long enough to see many of the changes that his Texas-tenor heralded.

The man who was known to his fellow musicians as "Jacket" was born Jean Baptiste Illinois Jacquet in Broussard, Louisiana in 1922, and was unique among famous jazz musicians in that his father was Creole and his mother a Sioux Indian. He got the name Illinois because a relative of his mother's went down to Louisiana to help with the birth. When he was very young he, along with his five brothers and sisters, moved to Texas, where he grew up in Houston. His father played bass in a railroad company band, and as a child Illinois would play music with his father's part-time band, along with his older brother Russell, a trumpet-player (who later played with the Cotton Club's house band in the late 1940s), and his brother Linton, who played the drums.

Illinois started out as a soprano saxophonist, and also learned the bassoon as a child. By the age of fifteen he was already playing with local bands run by Lionel Proctor, Bob Cooper and Milton Larkins around the Houston area. Sometime around 1940 he moved to the West Coast via Kansas City, where he jammed with Charlie Parker. In Los Angeles he met Nat King Cole and sometimes sat in with his trio at the Radio Room. It was on one of these occasions that he met Lionel Hampton who had also come up to jam with the King Cole Trio. Jacquet found a regular gig with the Floyd Ray Orchestra, before switching to Lionel Hampton's band in 1941.

Illinois Jacquet, New York, ca. May 1947.

In December 1941 Illinois made his first recording with the Hampton band who were in the studio in New York to cut four sides. Illinois can be heard on tenor sax, having been asked by Hampton to switch from the soprano because that's what the band was short of. As well as the nineteen-year-old Jacquet, Dexter Gordon can be heard on tenor, with Jack McVea on baritone sax. Three months later, the Hampton band were back in the studio recording four more sides. Among them was a song called "Flying Home" that Hampton had arranged, and it was this record that made young Illinois' reputation. Not that this was the first time that Hampton had recorded the tune – back in 1940 he did another version, with Ziggy Elman on trumpet, but it's the 1942 version that everyone remembers, mostly because of Jacquet's honking horn.

"If you can't tap your feet, something's wrong." ~ Illinois Jacquet

The record has many of the trademarks of rock'n'roll – some have even called it the first rock'n'roll record – but they are missing the point. "Flying Home" is jazz, but jazz of a new and very different kind.

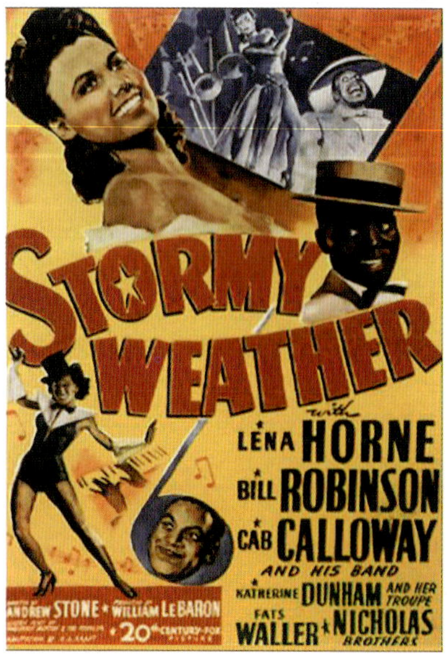

In 1943 Jacquet left Hampton to join Cab Calloway's Orchestra. Calloway's band had been a high-profile fixture on the fun end of jazz throughout the thirties, and along with Ellington, did much to ease the way for other black performers on national radio. By 1943 his best years had past, but the band was still a big attraction, having had a hit in 1942 with "Blues In the Night," featuring Dizzy Gillespie on trumpet. By the time Illinois joined the band, Dizzy had left, having been falsely accused of stabbing his boss in the leg while they were on stage. Shortly after Jacquet joined Calloway, the band appeared in the film *Stormy Weather* with Lena Horne. It also featured Fats Waller performing "Ain't Misbehavin'; the film came out just five months before Waller's tragic death aged just thirty-nine.

By the following year, Illinois was back in California. Among the many musical forays he made while living in Hollywood was an appearance in a short film called *Jammin' The Blues*. Among those featured were Harry "Sweets" Edison, Jo Jones, Lester Young and a twenty-one-year old Barney Kessel on guitar. Kessel was the only white musician to appear in the short, although no one watching it was aware of his color. His face is never shown in the full light, he's seated in the shadows; and they stained his hands with berry juice to make them appear black for close-ups of his guitar-playing . What makes this film so interesting is that it was a jam session, and few, if any, had ever been filmed before.

Not long after making *Jammin' the Blues,* Jacquet formed his own group, one that included his brother Russell on trumpet and twenty-two-year-old Charlie Mingus, the bass player who had recently toured with Louis Armstrong's Orchestra and appeared on one of Russell Jacquet's recordings for Globe Records earlier in the year. The Illinois Jacquet All Stars, as they were most subtly billed, recorded in Hollywood in August 1945 for the Apollo label. Besides his brother and Mingus, the pianist Bill Doggett, who would later have a big hit on the *Billboard* charts with "Honky Tonk," was also there. It was a busy day for the musicians as they also backed Wynonie Harris on a couple of sides. "Wynonie's Blues" subsequently became a Top 3 hit on the Harlem Hit Parade published each week in *Billboard*. By the following

Illinois Jacquet, New York, c. May 1947.

"Mr. Jacquet is the real thing." ~ The New York Times

month, *Billboard* went one step further and called it the Race Records Chart before they settled on the Rhythm and Blues Records Chart in 1949. "Wynonie's Blues" was much more like a rock'n'roll record than "Flyin' Home." At the end of the month the All Stars were back in the studio with largely the same group of musicians, although Johnny Otis was on drums; Otis, who was in the throes of forming his own band, would also become very successful.

Late in 1945 Jacquet moved back east to New York City, where he joined the Count Basie Orchestra,

replacing Lester Young; it was only a short stint as he left the following year but he remained living in Queens, which became his home for the rest of his life. Jacquet once joked that he lived in Queens because you could buy a home there for what it cost to park your car in Manhattan. Illinois soon reformed his All Stars and began touring and recording regularly. In 1947 he made his second appearance with Jazz at the Philharmonic, having been among the musicians to appear at the first one in 1944. For his first appearance he played alongside his old friends Nat King Cole, Jack McVea and Les Paul. Come the 1947 JATP show at New York's Carnegie Hall, Illinois was working with Howard McGhee on trumpet and Hank Jones on piano, among the all-star line up, playing "Perdido," "Mordido" and "Endido." Jacquet went on to appear in several more JATP shows, where his dueling saxophone exchanges with Flip Phillips invariably brought the house down.

Among his numerous recording sessions in the late 1940s and early 1950s was one in 1952 on which Count Basie plays organ on several sides. Throughout this period, brother Russell was often to be found working with Illinois. There were times in the mid-1950s that Jacquet expanded his small group to play on larger theater dates. In the 1960s and 1970s he toured Europe frequently, often working with The Texas Tenors, who included Arnett Cobb and Buddy Tate. He also experimented with the bassoon, using it to great effect on "Round Midnight," a 1969 recording by Thelonious Monk.

In 1983 he received an invitation from Harvard to conduct a series of master classes, and he later became an artist-in-residence at the university. He found that while his students had a great interest in the music of the big bands, they knew very little about them and their history.

"Jazz music is deeper than people think. It is a spiritual form of art. It's like a Picasso painting. There's no such thing as art going out of style."
~ Illinois Jacquet

Russell Jacquet, trumpet; Leo Parker, baritone sax and Illinois Jacquet, tenor sax, New York, c. May 1947.

This inspired Jacquet to put together a group of musicians to perpetuate the big-band sound – the Illinois Jacquet Big Band was very much in the style of Count Basie, but naturally, they always played "Flyin' Home."

He played at the White House for both presidents Jimmy Carter and Ronald Reagan, before the Illinois Jacquet Big Band was invited to perform at Bill Clinton's Inaugural Ball In January 1993. Among those who played with Jacquet's band were Grover Washington Jr., Thelonious Monk Jr., Herbie Hancock, Wayne Shorter, Clark Terry and President Clinton. An amateur saxophonist himself, Clinton performed "C-Jam Blues" with Jacquet.

In later years, as the depth and quality of his musicianship became better understood, he was elevated to the status of one of the most respected elder statesmen of jazz. As well as performing for eight decades, Jacquet also composed more than 300 tunes, the best known of which are "Black Velvet," "Robbins" Nest" and "Port of Rico." Houston Person, a fellow saxophonist summed up Illinois Jacquet career. "He was a great balladeer – I would say one of the greatest. He just never got the credit he deserved."

Illinois Jacquet, New York, c. May 1947.

ILLINOIS JACQUET

BORN October 31, 1922 in Broussard, LA

DIED July 22, 2004 in Queens, New York, NY

INSTRUMENT Tenor Saxophone

FIRST RECORDED 1941

INFLUENCES Herschel Evans, Lester Young, Coleman Hawkins

RECOMMENDED LISTENING

Illinois Jacquet Collates (1956)

Port of Rico (1958)

The Blues, That's Me (1969)

Jacquet's Got It (1989)

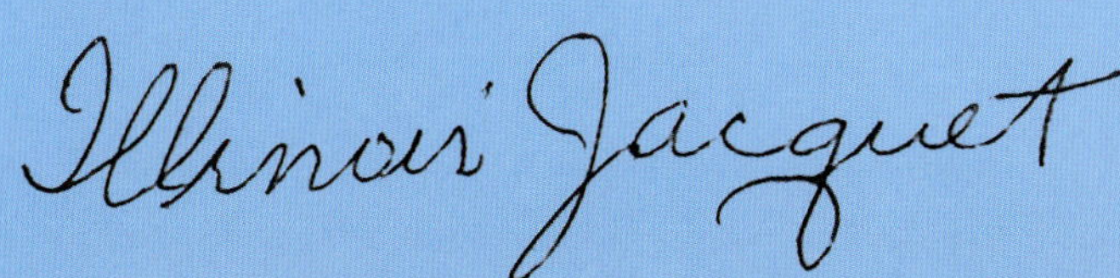

Art Pepper

"You couldn't file him in a category. He wasn't L.A. cool, white bop, '50s or '80s, but an impassioned musician with an alto sax and a rhythm section that never completely satisfied him. Despite the facile clichés of the music he mastered, he made you know that, facility and clichés notwithstanding, no one else could ever play like that." *~ Gary Giddins, author*

Art Pepper was different. He didn't come from the Deep South like many of the early jazz players, nor did he come from Chicago or Kansas City, instead he came from the Golden State. He was to be in on the birth of a new kind of cool – California Cool. As one reviewer once said, "He's an architect of emotion."

Arthur Edward Pepper Jr was born in September 1925 in Gardena, a suburb of Los Angeles. His father was a longshoreman in the port and was sometimes away from home working as a seaman. By all accounts Art was an unwanted child, which may, in part, explain some of what happened later. Initially he learned to play the clarinet when he was nine years old, then switched to the alto saxophone when he was thirteen.

In 1943, while Art was still a teenager, he played briefly with Gus Arnheim's Orchestra, before joining Benny Carter's band. Carter had relocated from New York early in the year having decided to try his luck in Los Angeles. Art also played with Stan Kenton in the same year, recording "Harlem Folk Dance" with the band. However, like many men his age, and many of the men playing with the big bands he was called up; he joined the Army and became a military policeman.

Once home from the war, Pepper worked briefly with a band called the Modern Jazz Stars, before picking up where he left off, rejoining the Kenton band, and drummer Shelly Manne joined around the same time. They and the other Kenton band members enjoyed great success as they played the amazing Pete Rugolo arrangements that characterized the orchestra in the postwar years. Business was good for the Kenton band – they won the Band of the Year award in the *Metronome* poll, which gives a good idea of the quality of the music that Pepper was playing. He was already an outstanding saxophonist and Kenton featured

Art Pepper in concert, 1947 or 1948.

SHELLY

him as a soloist on both gigs and on record.

Besides playing with Kenton, Pepper also freelanced and recorded with Eddie Safranski and the Poll Cats, the Bob Gonzales Orchestra, Charlie Mingus' 22-Piece Be Bop Band, and Maynard Ferguson's Orchestra; Ferguson had played trumpet in Kenton's band. There is a tremendous dichotomy in Pepper's time with the Stan Kenton Orchestra. They were undoubtedly one of the happiest periods of his life, but it was also when he became hooked on heroin. His addiction became a defining aspect of Art's life and career.

In 1951, when the Kenton band broke up, Pepper and many of the other Californians in the band decided that they wanted to stay on the coast; they wanted to live and work in California. Maybe they had just had enough of those Kenton check jackets and the regimen of life on a band bus. Shorty Rogers, Shelly Manne, Bud Shank and Milt Bernhart (who later played on numerous Frank Sinatra records for Capitol including the stunning trombone solo on "I've Got You Under My Skin"), all went back to Los Angeles. All these jazzmen would have a hand in creating the sound of California Cool. Initially, it was hard for them to find work – most club owners in Los Angeles were more interested in Dixieland than anything that sounded even slightly modern.

Pepper and the rest of them played some pretty awful stuff just to earn a living. It was often a case of weddings or Latin American music – take your pick. The Lighthouse Café on Pier Avenue in Hermosa Beach had begun putting

"He is an eloquent and gifted man." *~ Whitney Balliett in the* New Yorker

Stan Kenton, Eddie Safranski, Bob Cooper, Art Pepper, Ray Wetzel, Chico Alvarez, Harry Betts, and Shelly Manne, Richmond, VA, 1947 or 1948.

on jazz in 1949, and by 1951 Howard Rumsey became part-owner of the club as well as its manager. The first thing he did was to form the Lighthouse all Stars to feature on the modern jazz nights and especially at weekends. Before long, Art along with his old Kenton band mates, was playing there regularly.

Pepper played the odd session with fellow Kenton alumni Shorty Rogers's Giants in October 1951, as well as with the Shelly Manne's Septet. In January 1952 Pepper came second to Charlie Parker in the *Downbeat* Readers' Poll for best alto saxophonist. This coincided with his decision to start his own group, and on January 6, 1952 the Art Pepper Septet were recorded at the Lighthouse Club. Rogers, Manne and Bernhart were all there, along with Howard Rumsey, the club's owner on bass, Jimmy Giuffre on tenor sax and Frank Patchen on piano.

In March 1952 Pepper went into a studio in Los Angeles to record for the Discovery label. He cut "Surf Ride," one of his best cuts, along with a beautiful version of "These Foolish Things." In 1953 he recorded more sides for Discovery, as well as working with Shorty Rogers and Shelley Manne. In August 1954 Pepper was back in the studio with his Quartet, but it was to be his last session for some time as his increasing problems with heroin resulted in him being sent to prison for nearly two years.

On his release, he was soon back working with old friend Shorty Rogers, playing with his Giants, along with trumpeters, Harry "Sweets" Edison, Maynard Ferguson; Milt Bernhart and Jimmy Giuffre were also there. Eager to make up for lost time Pepper worked with his own band,

Shelly Manne, Art Pepper, and Bob Gioga, 1947 or 1948.

"He had the notes, and he was swinging all the time. That's very important... Art always swung. And he played all the instruments... exactly the same. He put them in his mouth and it was Art Pepper." ~ *Marty Paich*

and also did some sessions with Chet Baker. There were the first of his sessions with pianist Marty Paich, which was to prove an enduring and fruitful relationship. He even did an album with Hoagy Carmichael.

A session in January 1957 produced the first real standout album of his career – *Art Pepper Meets the Rhythm Section*. The section being Red Garland on piano, Paul Chambers on bass, and drummer Philly Joe Jones. There's a great deal of legend surrounding this album. On the liner notes it says that Pepper hadn't played for two weeks before the session and only learned about it on the morning of the day they were to record. In fact, Pepper had played at least four sessions since the turn of the year, so that part of the story is clearly unreliable. What is probably true is that Pepper had never met the other three musicians. Whatever the truth, the results are amazing and this album would do much to seal Pepper's reputation with a growing audience.

Over the next two years Art worked with Mel Torme, Herb Ellis, Barney Kessel, June Christy and Pete Rugolo from his Kenton days, and Henry Mancini, as well as sessions with Marty Paich's orchestra. One of his recordings with Paich is justifiably considered a classic, not just among Pepper's work, but also in jazz as a whole. *Art Pepper + Eleven* was recorded between March and May 1959. It features superb arrangements and some of Pepper's best playing; it's been called "high art" and should be in every jazz fan's library.

On January 20, 1961 Pepper backed singer Helyne Stewart at a session with the Teddy Edwards Septet, it was Pepper's last for nearly three years, before he was sent to prison again for his heroin use. This time it was San Quentin. Ironically, he had recently recorded a track called "Smack Up," which became the title of the album released while he was in jail. There's no indication on the album of a man who was probably in a bad way. It's so difficult to reconcile the addiction with the music, but for non-addicts trying to fathom the mind of an addict is close to impossible.

After his release from San Quentin, Pepper deserted his old style and for a while played a much freer kind of jazz. He also went back to prison for another spell in 1965 and then was not heard on record again until 1968, when he went back to what he knew best – jazz with a big band. He joined Buddy Rich and during his short time with them he made one album – *Mercy, Mercy*.

Pepper was not in good shape. After working with his own quintet for a short time at Donte's in North Hollywood, he quit the music business altogether. He spent three years in rehab while working as a bookkeeper. It wasn't until 1973 that Pepper began working again, initially as a demonstrator for Buffet, the saxophone maker. In 1975 Art returned to the studio to record under his own name. Later in the year he did an album with old friend Shelly Manne and pianist Hampton Hawes, with Charlie Haden on bass. Pepper was fifty; with his lifestyle and history there was a hint of irony in the album's title – *Living Legend*.

Over the next few years he continued to record with his own band, but he also worked with Art Farmer and vibraphonist, Cal Tjader. There were a series of stunning live shows at the Village Vanguard in New York City, the Newport Jazz Festival, as well as in Japan. Pepper was back, receiving plaudits and the kind of recognition that his use of drugs had probably denied him.

In 1980 he visited the UK with pianist, Milcho Leviev and played at Ronnie Scott's Club. The next year he undertook an extensive tour of Britain in his own name, and played to packed houses; he also played in Europe and enjoyed similar success.

Art Pepper was a man who had more than his fair share of demons, but to listen to much of his music you would imagine this is the sweetest, most mellow man on the planet. While he is inexorably linked to the West Coast Jazz scene, he was a much harder, more direct player than many of his contemporaries. When he took up the tenor saxophone during his "free jazz" period, it showed a man who was interested in exploring his musical possibilities. However, Art Pepper returned to his alto and left a legacy of great jazz saxophone recordings that few can match.

Much of the credit for Pepper's return to form in the seventies is probably due to his marriage to Laurie, his third wife. She appears to have been a stabilizing influence on a man who was certainly in need of it. Pepper died in 1982 after a stroke.

ART PEPPER

BORN September 1, 1925 in Gardena, CA

DIED June 1, 1982 in Panorama City, CA

INSTRUMENT Alto Sax, briefly the tenor sax

FIRST RECORDED 1943

INFLUENCES Charlie Parker, Benny Carter, Stan Kenton

RECOMMENDED LISTENING

Art Pepper Meets the Rhythm Section *(1957)*

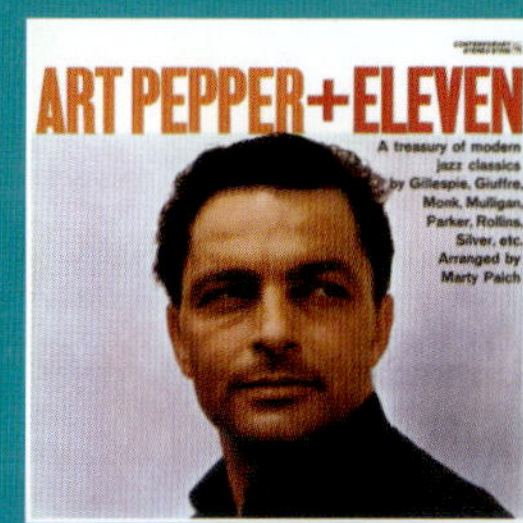

Art Pepper + Eleven *(1959)*

Smack Up *(1960)*

Straight Life *(1979)*

MILES DAVIS

"To be and stay a great musician you've got to always be open to what's new, what's happening at the moment."
~ Miles Davis

He was man of contradictions, sometimes angry and arrogant, and on other occasions generous and introspective. He was also a genius who discovered and encouraged others. His haunting tone and constantly changing style allowed him to become involved in just about anything and everything that happened in modern jazz. His unique playing style, with its voice-like quality and tone that was almost free of vibrato, could sometimes be melancholy, at others times assertive. It helped to make him the model for generations of jazz musicians and, for jazz lovers the world over, Miles Davis defined cool.

Here was another jazzman that came, not from the poor sided of town, but from affluence. His father was a dentist and a year after Miles Dewey Davis III was born in May 1926, in Alton, Illinois, the family moved to East St. Louis. For his thirteenth birthday Miles was given a trumpet and lessons with a local jazz musician named Elwood Buchanan. By the age of fifteen he had already got his musicians' union card, allowing him to play around St. Louis with Eddie Randall's Blue Devils.

In 1944 the newly formed Billy Eckstine Band arrived in St. Louis, and their third trumpet player was unwell, so Miles was able to sit in with the band for their two-week engagement. The Eckstine band was already creating a proto-be-bop sound, thanks to two of its members, alto saxophonist, Charlie Parker and Dizzy Gillespie, who was also the band's musical director. The experience for eighteen-year-old Miles was life-changing. He decided to move to New York, the epicentre of the be-bop revolution, to immerse himself in their dogma. Having persuaded his less than enthusiastic parents that a career in music was what he wanted, he enrolled at the Juilliard School of Music and began studying classical music in September 1944. Miles spent his evenings and nights in the clubs of Harlem and 52nd Street, studying jazz and playing whenever he could find a band to sit in with.

He made his first recording at WOR studios, two blocks from Times Square, on April 24, 1945 backing a singer named, Rubberlegs Williams, on what were more pop songs than jazz. In the autumn he joined Charlie Parker's quintet, which included Dizzy Gillespie; they

Charlie Parker and Miles Davis at the Three Deuces, New York, c. August 1947.

recorded in November when they were billed as the Bee-Boppers. This also coincided with the end of Miles's sojourn at the Julliard; he left to become a fully-fledged jazzman, a fact that his parents, apparently, accepted somewhat reluctantly.

The November session yielded the single, "Now's the Time," coupled with "Billie's Bounce," the first fully formed be-bop record. In the early part of 1946, Davis headed out to Los Angeles with the Parker band and they recorded a number of sides for the Dial label, as well as playing clubs that included The Finale in Hollywood. Miles also played with Charles Mingus's band on a session, and worked with Benny Carter and Billy Eckstine's orchestras.

By the beginning of 1947 Miles was back in New York recording with Illinois Jacquet, but he also continued to work with Charlie Parker, as well as playing a session with Coleman Hawkins' All Stars. Having gained a good deal of experience with others, he made his first recording as a leader on August 14 1947, with a quintet that included Parker on tenor sax, John Lewis on piano, bassist Nelson Boyd, and Max Roach on the drums.

By the middle of 1948, after numerous sessions with Parker's band, Miles was showing the restless side of his musical character and wanted to try new things, moving away from what he perhaps saw as the constraints of be-bop. What Miles did next was the genesis of what we've come to call, "cool jazz." It was also the start of Davis working with the arranger Gil Evans, who would become a frequent collaborator throughout his career. Evans was thirty-six and already had a reputation for adventurous arranging. It was his ability to arrange skillfully so as to create the impression of a big band, while still maintaining the dexterity of a small group, that particularly appealed to Miles.

"If you listen to the music, there's no rage. There's love, there's vulnerability."
~ Herbie Hancock

The Miles Davis Nonet or Orchestra, as it was sometimes billed, got a residency at the Royal Roost in New York, which also enabled them to broadcast on the radio. With future MJQ member, John Lewis on piano, and Gerry Mulligan on baritone sax among the guiding spirits of this band, it proved to be a highly creative unit. When they finally went into the studio in January 1949 to record for Capitol Records, it was Lewis' arrangements that they recorded. A few months later they were back, this time with Gil Evans' arrangements. Another session in March 1950 was all that the band managed, but this really was the "birth of the cool."

The importance of these sessions, and the records

"I always listen to what I can leave out." *~ Miles Davis*

Miles Davis and Howard McGhee, New York, c. September 1947.

"Miles conceived these settings only hours before the recording dates." ~ Bill Evans on Kind of Blue

they produced, are immense. They really were the epitome of cool, intimate records that oozed sophistication for an audience that was looking towards a new world order after the austerity of war. These recordings inspired the West Coast cool jazz sound from which so many sub genres became the direct descendants.

While musically these records were not as well received at their first release, they set Davis on a course that he stuck to over the rest of the decade. In the immediate aftermath of these sessions, while Miles continued to record, he did so with some lesser sidemen for the next three years or so. He had become a heroin addict, which meant that he performed much less often than he had previously.

In 1954 he kicked his habit and began working on what would become the first phase of his small-group recordings. He worked with Art Blakey, Horace Silver, Kenny Clarke, Sonny Rollins, Milt Jackson and Thelonious Monk; it was a sure sign that Miles was back. One of the foremost releases from this period is the album *Bags Groove,* which displayed Miles's brilliance alongside Sonny Rollins and Horace Silver. It has been described as a cornerstone of any jazz collection, and it richly deserves its place in the Davis' canon, although it sometimes gets overlooked for some of the later albums.

The following year Miles appeared at the Newport Jazz Festival, where his playing was rapturously received by both the fans and the press. In the wake of this performance Miles established a quintet that included pianist Red Garland, Paul Chambers on bass, Philly Joe Jones on drums and John Coltrane on tenor saxophone. This is the group that made *Round Midnight,* the album that re-established Miles's reputation as a live performer throughout the best jazz venues in America.

In autumn of 1956 Miles worked with the Jazz and Classical Music Society on an interesting collaboration arranged by John Lewis. Miles not only played trumpet, but also the flugelhorn, showing a side of his playing that had hitherto been largely hidden. It was like a clarion call for what followed. In May 1957 Gil Evans created some stunning arrangements for a jazz orchestra, which would eventually become the album *Miles Ahead.* It includes "The Maids Of Cadiz," a piece

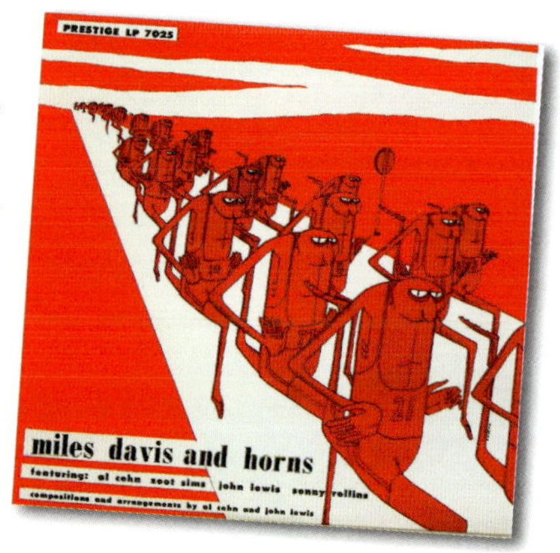

written by Delibes; this was the first piece of classical music that Miles recorded. In 1958 he made an album of Gershwin's *Porgy and Bess,* following this with *Sketches of Spain* in 1959; here he plays works by Rodrigo and De Falla. It includes the "Concerto de Aranjuez" a tour-de-force by Miles against a sumptuous Gil Evans setting.

Just prior to recording the "Concerto de Aranjuez," the Miles Davis Sextet recorded what is, for just about everybody, his greatest album and arguably one of the half dozen most important records of the twentieth century. Besides Miles, Coltrane and Chambers there were his new pianist Bill Evans, Cannonball Adderley on alto sax and Jimmy Cobb plays drums. The album was recorded over two sessions and pivots not only around Miles's brilliant playing, but also that of classically trained Bill Evans. From its opening track, "So What," it heralds a new kind of jazz.

For the next five years Miles worked with many of the same musicians, although Bill Evans had left to pursue his own kind of exploratory jazz, and Wynton Kelly was at the piano, along with Sonny Stitt on alto sax on a very successful European tour in 1960. In the early sixties others who appeared with the various incarnations of the Davis' group included, Hank Mobley and Wayne Shorter on tenor sax, Victor Feldman and Herbie Hancock on piano, Ron Carter on bass and Tony Williams on drums. As well as playing with the band, Shorter also contributed some stand-out compositions, including "Nefertiti" and "Footprints."

The Shorter, Hancock, Carter, Williams group is known as the "second great quintet"; it was also the last of Davis's purely acoustic line-ups. By the late sixties Miles

"A legend is an old man with a cane known for what he used to do. I'm still doing it."
~ Miles Davis

"Probably left the biggest hole we'll ever know in twentieth-century music." ~ Quincy Jones

was including electric bass and piano, as well as guitar on his recordings, which were a much freer form of jazz. Everything was pointing towards the fusion sound that would come to dominate his playing. In 1969 for the *In A Silent Way* album the band included John McLaughlin on guitar, Chick Corea on keyboards, Joe Zawinul on organ and Dave Holland on bass, along with Shorter, Hancock and Williams. This proved to be something of a stepping-stone towards what happened next.

Bitches Brew was an historic breakthough with its jazz-fusion, in which elements of rock were meshed with the jazz idiom. This new style allowed the musicians a much broader creative canvas. Harvey Brooks was added on electric bass, Billy Cobham played drums, as did Jack DeJohnette. These, plus others, whose background was as much rock as it was jazz, created a Miles Davis sound that introduced the trumpeter, whose instrument was electrified for this album, to a whole new generation of fans. It was about as far from "cool" as could be, but it sold 500,000 double albums and became his best ever selling record – although *Kind of Blue* is possibly catching up following the advent of the CD.

From here on, over the next few years, Miles continued to experiment with fusion jazz, introducing Keith Jarrett into the small group, along with percussionist, Airto Moreira. But just as he was continuing to evolve and reinvent his sound, he broke both his legs in a car accident. It was the start of some difficult health problems that plagued him for the rest of his life. He had diabetes, problems with a hip joint that was attributed to sickle-cell anemia, and he had pneumonia that seemed to go on and on. His temperament, which was far from even, may also have been affected by his use of cocaine. He recorded in March 1976 and that was the last time he worked in the 1970s.

Miles began working again in 1980, recording properly in 1981, but in February 1982 he suffered a mild stroke. In April 1982 he toured Britain and Europe, before returning to America and the recording studio. He continued to record for Columbia until he had a fairly public spat with trumpeter Wynton Marsalis that ended in the label dropping Miles and putting a lot of money behind the "new jazz" of Marsalis. Miles even worked with some of the new wave of British rock acts, proving he was still keen to be trying new things, even if they were not always musically fulfilling for anyone involved.

In 1987 he recorded an album entitled *Tutu* that exploited modern studio techniques and instruments; it also won him a Grammy. It is the last really significant recording of Miles's long career. He had mellowed somewhat, and was less irascible than during the height of his fame. According to his former drummer, Max Roach who was battling alcoholism with treatment paid for by Miles, "He was the most generous person." Roach only found out that Miles was paying after he got a message while he was in rehab to say, "Tell Max that he's gotta get himself together 'cause he's costing too much money."

Miles Davis's last performance was in August 1991 at

Charlie Parker and Miles Davis at the Three Deuces, New York, c. August 1947.

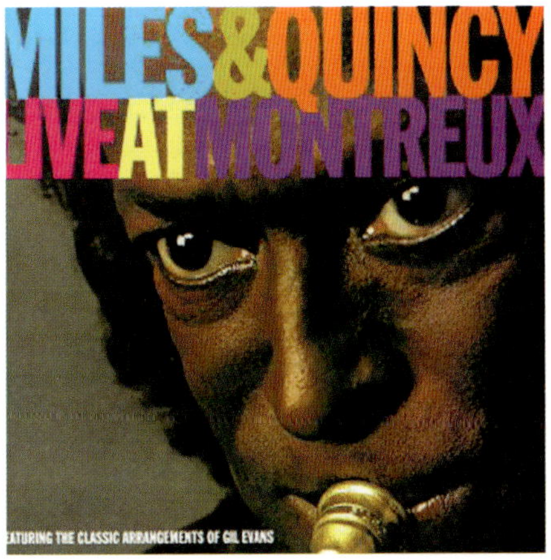

the Hollywood Bowl in California, having just returned from a tour in France and an appearance at the Montreux Jazz Festival with the Quincy Jones Orchestra. The man who had once said, "I have to change; it's like a curse," died in September 1991 of pneumonia, respiratory failure and a stroke; he was sixty-five years old.

For days after he died jazz radio stations across America seemed to play his music almost continuously; they didn't come close to exhausting the supply. During his five decades of recording, from the end of World War Two to 1990, his output was prodigious. He recorded in seemingly every known style of jazz – except maybe New Orleans. He did 12-bar blues to full-length concerto-like pieces, and created music to suit every known human emotion and mood. Given the size of his output, it's amazing that so much of it is so good. In fact, there's a lot that is remarkable, and some of it is the best jazz that was ever put onto vinyl.

Howard McGhee and Miles Davis, New York, c. September 1947.

MILES DAVIS

BORN May 26, 1926 in Alton, IL

DIED September 28, 1991 in Santa Monica, CA

INSTRUMENT Trumpet

FIRST RECORDED 1945

INFLUENCES Clark Terry, Charlie Parker, Dizzy Gillespie

RECOMMENDED LISTENING

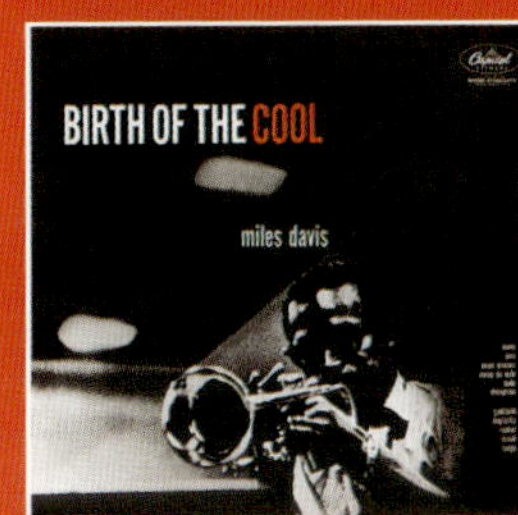

Birth of Cool *(1949/50)*

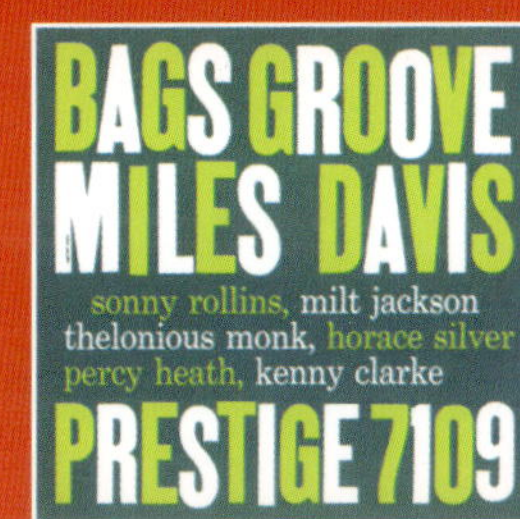

Bags Groove *(1957)*

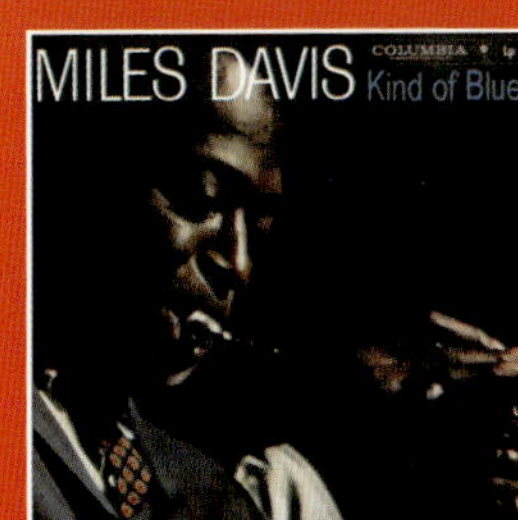

Kind of Blue *(1959)*

Sketches of Spain *(1960)*

Bitches Brew *(1970)*

THE MUSIC ON THE CD

1. **West End Blues** *(King Joe Oliver/Clarence Williams) Redwood Music Ltd/B. Feldman & Co Ltd.*
Louis Armstrong's Hot Five recorded this on Thursday June 28, 1928 in Chicago. Besides Louis' trumpet you hear Fred Robinson on trombone, Jimmy Strong on clarinet, Earl Hines on piano, Mancy Cara on banjo and Zutty Singleton on drums – it's sublime.

2. **Twinklin**' *(Mary Lou Williams) EMI Robbins Catalog.*
On February 8, 1938 Mary Lou Williams along with Andy Kirk & His Clouds of Joy went into a New York studio to let her fingers do the talking on a tune she both wrote and arranged.

3. **Take The 'A' Train** *(Billy Strayhorn) Billy Strayhorn Songs/Cherry Lane Music.*
Recorded by Duke Ellington and his Orchestra in Hollywood in February 1941, it soon became the band's signature tune and one of the most instantly recognizable jazz tunes of al time. Billy Strayhorn's writing and arranging was pivotal to the Duke's sound. Here the saxophones provide the perfect cushion for Ray Nance's trumpet playing.

4. **Body And Soul** *(John Green/Edward Heyman/Robert Sour) Druropetal Music.*
The Coleman Hawkins Orchestra recording of this jazz classic occurred at the end of a session in New York City on October 11, 1939… as an afterthought. Hawkins' tenor saxophone is perfection throughout and it is the perfect record to play to people who say they don't like jazz.

5. **One O'clock Jump** *(Count Basie /Harry James) EMI Feist Catalog Inc.*
The Count Basie Orchestra theme tune was recorded in New York City on July 7, 1937. The first of the sax solos is by Herschel Evans while the second is the incomparable Lester Young; his follows a trombone solo by George Hunt. Among the other members of the band are Freddie Green on guitar with Walter Page on bass and Joe Jones on drums.

6. **I'll Be Seeing You** *(Irving Kahal / Sammy Fain) Fain Music Co / Irving Kahal Music.*
Frank Sinatra recorded this at his fourth session with Tommy Dorsey & His Orchestra on February 26, 1940 and came out as the b-side of 'Polka Dots and Moonbeams', which the Dorsey band recorded a week later in the same RCA Studio 2 in New York City.

7. **Let Me Off Uptown** *(Evans Redd/Earl Bostic) MCA Duchess Music Corporation/Chappell and Co Ltd., (London)*
Recorded by the fifteen-piece Gene Krupa Orchestra on May 8, 1941 in New York City, it features the brilliant Roy Eldridge on trumpet and the great Anita O'Day on vocals. It epitomises much of what William Gottlieb's photography portrayed.

8. **Artistry in Rhythm** *(Stanley Kenton) EMI Robbins Catalog.*
Recorded at C.P. Macgregor Studios, Hollywood on November 19, 1943 this tune written and arranged by Stan Kenton came out on Capitol Records the following year. It made the charts as the b-side of 'Eager Beaver' and both tunes did so much to seal his reputation.

9. **Skyliner** *(Charlie Barnet) Atlantic Music Corp.*
The Charlie Barnet Orchestra recorded 'Skyliner' for the Decca label in 1944 and it would have probably have been a bigger hit if its release hadn't coincided with the ending of the war in Europe. Nevertheless it's a great tune and one of big band jazz's best recordings.

10. **Lover Man** *(Jimmy Davis/Roger Ramirex/Jimmy Sherman) Universal Music Corp.*
This beautiful song was specially written for Billie Holiday and she recorded it for Decca in 1945, it was her first recording for the label. The orchestra was arranged and conducted by Salvatore Camarata, who had been in the Jimmy Dorsey band, and it made number 5 on the *Billboard* Race Records chart in May.

11. **It's Only A Paper Moon** *(Harold Arlen / E.Y.Harburg / Billy Rose) Anne-Rachel Music/Glocca Morra Music.*
This song recorded by Ella Fitzgerald & The Delta Rhythm Boys made the Top 10 of the *Billboard* Best selling Popular Retail Records chart in the summer of 1945.

12. **Straight No Chaser** *(Thelonious Monk) Thelonious Music Corp.*
The Thelonious Monk session that produced this track was at WOR Studios in New York City on July 23, 1951. It was made by his Quintet that included Sahib Shihab on alto sax, Milt Jackson vibes, Al McKibbon on bass and Art Blakey on drums.

13. **Route 66** *(Bobby Troup) Troup London Music.*
Bobby Troup's inspiration for writing this classic song came after he and his wife drove from Lancaster, Pennsylvania to Los Angeles at the end of World War II. The King Cole Trio recorded it in 1946 for Capitol Records, Oscar Moore played guitar and Johnny Miller played bass; it made the *Billboard* Best Sellers chart in August of the same year.

14. **Rich-ual Fire Dance** *(Copyright Control).*
The Buddy Rich Orchestra recorded this great driving song for the Mercury label in 1946. It was released during his bop phase and failed to excite the record-buying public in America but as a testament to Buddy's brilliant drumming it certainly stands the test of time.

15. **Salt Peanuts** *(Kenneth Clarke / John Gillespie) Copyright Control.*
The Dizzy Gillespie Sextet recorded this bopper's anthem on January 9, 1945 in New York City. Besides Dizzy there's Trummy Young on trombone, Don Byas plays tenor sax, Clyde Hart the piano, Oscar Pettiford on bass and drummer, Irv Kluger.

16. **Misty** *(Erroll Garner/Johnny Burke) Marke Music / My Dad's Songs / Octave Music / Pocket Full of Dreams / Reganesque Music.*
Erroll Garner recorded this timeless classic on July 27, 1954 in Chicago; he apparently composed it in his head while he was flying into Chicago for the recording session. He recorded it in one take!

17. **Cool Blues** *(Charlie Parker) Songs of Universal Inc.*
Recorded by the Charlie Parker Quartet at C.P. Macgregor Studios, Hollywood on February 19, 1947, it had its initial release on the Dial label. Besides Parker's alto sax there's Erroll Garner on piano, Red Callender on bass and Doc west on drums.

18. **Flyin' Home** *(Benny Goodman/Lionel Hampton) Regent Music Corp.*
The Lionel Hampton Orchestra featuring Illinois Jacquet playing 'Flyin' Home' is a masterpiece of big-band jazz. Recorded on May 26, 1942 in New York City. Besides Jacquet there's Dexter Gordon on tenor sax and Jack McVea on baritone.

19. **You'd Be So Nice To Come Home To** *(Cole Porter) Chappell & Co. Inc.*
Recorded on January 19, 1957 in Hollywood, California by Art Pepper with the Rhythm Section this brilliant version of an old favourite features Red Garland on piano, bass player Paul Chambers and Philly Joe Jones on drums.

20. **Little Willie Leaps** *(Miles Davis) Screen Gems EMI Music.*
The Miles Davis All Stars recorded Little Willie Leaps at Harry Smith's Studios in New York City on August 14, 1947. The Stars being Charlie Parker on tenor sax, pianist John Lewis, Nelson Boyd on bass and Max Roach plays drums.

FURTHER READING

The Penguin Guide to Jazz Recordings
by Brian Morton and Richard Cook (2008) ISBN-10: 0141034017

The New Grove Dictionary of Jazz
by Barry D. Kernfeld (1994) ISBN-10: 0312113579

The Oxford Companion to Jazz
by Bill Kirchner (2005) ISBN-10: 0195183592

Encyclopedia of Jazz
by Leonard Feather (1960) ISBN-10: 0306802147

The Big Bands
by George T. Simon (1971) ISBN-10: 0026109700

Joel Whitburn's Pop Memories, 1890-1954: The History of American Popular Music (1986) ISBN-10: 0793508290

Jazz Writings
by Philip Larkin (2004) ISBN-10: 0826476996

For some of the best writing on jazz check out the Jazz Book Club which was founded in 1956. They reprinted many titles that had been released earlier; many of which are seminal works. First date is the one when the JBC published their version followed by the original publication date.

We Called it Music
by Eddie Condon & Thomas Sugrue (1956/1947)

Jazz in Perspective
by Iain Lang (1957/1947)

Jazzmen
Edited by Frederic Ramsey & Charles Edward Smith (1958/1939)

Jazz in Britain
by David Boulton (1959/1958)

The Jazz Scene
by Francis Newton (1960/1959)

Jam Session
Edited by Ralph Gleason (1960/1958)

The Book of Jazz
by Leonard Feather (1960/1957)

The Jazz Era - The Forties
Edited by Stanley Dance (1962/1961)

Blues Fell this Morning
by Paul Oliver (1963/1960)

Some of these titles have been reprinted or secondhand copies can be found at *www.addall.com* as can a whole host of great jazz writing long out of print.

For some brilliant live jazz DVDs go to *www.jazzicons.com* They are now on their third series of DVDs and feature some of the best concerts by the greatest performers over the last five decades.

Web sites
www.allaboutjazz.com
One of the most comprehensive web sites on jazz from every era.

www.jazzdisco.org
An online discography of jazz that is an amazing resource.

Always check on www.youtube.com as there are some fascinating historical performances, as well as more recent videos.

INDEX